M000305816

Notes in the Margin

Thirty Essays on Life and Faith

ELLEN L. FOELL

Notes in the Margin

Copyright © 2018 by Ellen L. Foell

No part of this publication may be reproduced, stored in a retrieval system, or transmitted, in any form or by any means—electronic, mechanical, photocopying, recording, or otherwise—except for brief quotations in critical reviews or articles, without the written prior permission of the author via ellen@ellenfoell.com.

Unless otherwise noted, Scriptures taken from the Holy Bible, New International Version®, NIV®. Copyright © 1973, 1978, 1984, 2011 by Biblica, Inc.™ Used by permission of Zondervan. All rights reserved worldwide. www. zondervan.com The "NIV" and "New International Version" are trademarks registered in the United States Patent and Trademark Office by Biblica, Inc.™

Notes in the Margin is a collection of essays. Some of them are reflections on Scripture passages that have impacted and helped me reinterpret my life. Others are memoir - recollections of public and private events that I have experienced directly. I share the people and facts of these events to the best of my ability with accuracy. Any and all interpretations of these events are solely my own.

Published by

FIREPOND
PRESS

Scottsville, Virginia, U.S.A.
firepondpress@gmail.com
www.firepondpress.com

The flame and wave logo is a trademark of Firepond Press. We are committed to coaching authors who tell stories that inspire their readers to "Wholeness, Boldness and Wonder."

Library of Congress Control Number: 2018902274 (Print)
First Edition
ISBN: 9780999220412

Printed in the United States of America

Notes in the Margin

To my Lord Jesus Christ,
who makes the work of writing
a wonderful and joyful effort.

Preface

You can't live long in this world before you encounter some circumstance that surprises you or makes you uncomfortable. This is true from our first dirty diaper all the way through adolescence into senior adulthood and the dreaded Depend.®

Life's circumstances delight me, challenge me, surprise or inspire me, disappoint, hurt, or heal me. Over the years, some things left me reeling from shock, conversations confused me, and experiences filled my heart with joy or, at other times, pain. Every day I have a choice to let the circumstances and attendant emotions master me or serve me. This happens for me, and for all of us.

Through it all, Truth guides me. It keeps me steady through all of the circumstances in life. The circumstances and my feelings about those circumstances have come and gone. The pain and delight ebbed and flowed. Truth has remained. Therefore, every day, I try to interpret life in the context of Truth. Otherwise, life and its spectrum of experiences become random and meaningless.

Truth matters. It makes a difference in the way life is lived, in the way we respond to fortune and misfortune. It matters into eternity because Truth outlasts today and tomorrow. Truth lasts, while today's circumstances, pain, delight, and challenges will not last into eternity.

Every day. Truth. Matters.

These essays peek into my daily life and how Truth has mattered in living life. It is my hope that as you read *Notes in the Margin* you will, indeed, find that every day Truth matters. As you discover Truth in these notes of mine, I invite you to write some of your own notes in the margins.

Contents

Notes in the Margin

I did not appreciate the value of margins until many years ago when I learned to speak and read elementary Thai. Because the language has five tones, it is not an easy language to speak. Moreover, it is not an easy language to read with its confusing script. You can imagine my bewilderment and sense of overwhelming stupidity when I first looked at the following page with my Khruu (teacher):

ในปฐมกาลพระวาทะทรงดำรงอยู่ และพระวาทะทรงอยู่กับพระเจ้า
และพระวาทะทรงเป็นพระเจ้า 2พระองค์ทรงอยู่กับพระเจ้าตั้งแต่ปฐมกาล
3สรรพสิ่งถูกสร้างขึ้นโดยทางพระองค์ นบรรดาสิ่งที่ถูกสร้างขึ้นมานั้น

The beauty of the script aside, written Thai has no periods, no paragraphs, and no commas. It proved very difficult for me to learn to read Thai simply because there is not enough white space. There isn't enough margin. I did not know when to start or stop.

I like margins. I need margins. In books, margins give me room to annotate. In my closet, margins give me room to add one pair of dress pants without having to knock out a wall. In my weight, margin gives me room to eat a little dessert now and again rather than to forgo completely. In my house, it gives me ability to find things easily and find a place for the thing I am not ready to part with. In scheduling, it allows room for the spontaneous visit or cup of coffee with a friend. In my thirty-plus-year-old Bible, margins give me the room to comment and wonder. In relationships, it leaves room for growth and change, my own and that of the other person. In my mind, margin is the silence that allows me to process, think, and reflect.

The western culture I live in seems to have a cultural aversion to margins. The airlines, as an example, typically overbook flights on the off chance that a passenger fails to show up for the flight. Hoarders can't emotionally get rid of anything, and so their dwelling places become so cluttered, there is no room left to move or sit. Some people pack schedules with "must-dos" beyond what could reasonably be accomplished in a lifetime, let alone a week. Thus, they are constantly late, no-shows, or making excuses. Cell phones, smart phones, laptops, iP-ads, tablets, cars, and coffee shops offer us opportunity to slavishly check the electronic devices every second that is not "wasted" talking face to face, or worse, while talking face to face. The devices cram our minds so full of information, useless and useful, that we cannot remember a loved one's birthday without four reminders, three days before, one day before, one hour before, and fifteen minutes before. The coffee shops that used to be places to comfortably and leisurely connect, have now become places where we can get plugged in, logged on, and tuned out from the person with whom we came to the coffee shop.

What is the fuss? Why do I lament about societal and my own acceptance of marginless life and communication? Why do I struggle so hard to set and keep margins, in spite of supposedly thriving on a cluttered, last-minute life? Primarily because, as I have spent time writing and collecting these essays, I understand where *Notes in the Margin* came from. These essays came from the intentional time I carved out to create margin in my schedule and in my mind. These essays came from relentlessly pounding out three miles at the gym, where I not only run, but think. The essays emanate from the margins in my Bible, where I have annotated the seed form of some of these essays. They come from the margin in my schedule that allows me to run back and forth to care for my aging parents. They come from sitting around with my friend every Monday evening talking and then reflecting. (Someday I will learn to reflect and then speak.) These essays came from observing life and taking the time to write down those observations and reflections. They came from sitting in the dark, as well as the light. And thinking.

I need margins. However, even after 59 years, I have yet to encounter the job, the schedule, the children, the spouse, or the food craving that offered margin before the tyrannical enjoyment or press of the moment. The only way to enjoy margins is to define them and then fight for them. Of course, then I fill them with more notes.

Amazing Jesus

LUKE 7

How amazing Jesus is! But here's a question: What amazed Jesus? The Bible tells me that when Jesus traversed this dusty earth, two things amazed him: the presence of faith and the absence of faith.

In Luke 7:1-6 there is a story of a Gentile centurion whose servant was very ill. The centurion had heard of Jesus and sent some of the Jewish elders to ask Jesus to come and heal the servant. The elders begged Jesus to go on the basis of the man's great contributions to the Jewish people.

The centurion had built a synagogue for the Jews. It impressed the Jews. Did it amaze Jesus? Did the fact that the centurion had a great affection for the people of Israel impress Jesus? What about the centurion's position over a hundred Roman soldiers? No, those things neither impressed nor amazed Jesus.

The centurion served in the Roman army, yet was a man of compassion. He valued his servant highly and was willing to humble himself to plead for the elders' help. He didn't order anyone to ask Jesus. He didn't command Jesus to come into his presence. He asked. Asking is a sign of humility. Jesus responded and went. However, before Jesus got to the centurion's house, the centurion again sent word to Jesus that he did not need to come. Instead, he invited Jesus to "say the word." The centurion had a good idea of his own authority, Caesar's authority and the authority of Jesus.

> When Jesus heard this, he was amazed at
> him, and turning to the crowd following
> him, he said, "I tell you, I have not found
> such great faith even in Israel" (Luke 7:9).

The centurion got it. From the centurion's dissertation on authority it was clear that he understood the authority of Jesus and trusted his authority completely, even with the life of his servant.

That is critical for me. Faith is more than my personal submission to Jesus' authority. It requires acting on the understanding that everything and everyone is under his authority. The centurion understood that, within his limited little human kingdom of soldiers, he had authority. Not as much authority as Caesar did, but, he had authority.

When Caesar told the centurion to go somewhere, the centurion went without question, without hesitation, without delay. But this Jesus, his authority was over sickness, over disease, over lameness and over deafness. This Jesus had unequaled authority. Therefore, the centurion pleaded, "But say the word, and I know he will be healed." Jesus was amazed and told the crowd this type of faith was rare. Not even in the house of Israel had Jesus seen such faith.

Another time, while visiting his hometown, Jesus was again amazed, not by the presence of faith, but by its absence. In Mark 6:6, Jesus did the same things he had been doing in Nazareth and Jerusalem: he preached in the synagogue, and many who heard him were amazed. However, many who heard were not amazed. In fact, they referred to him derisively as "this man" as they asked, "Who is this man?" They questioned his actions because they doubted his authority. How could the ability and the power to perform miracles find its home in such a humble carpenter, the son of Mary, the adulteress, pregnant when she was betrothed? The son of Joseph the carpenter? How could Jesus have such authority? How dare he? He has no right to have such authority. And so, Jesus could do only a few miracles, and he was amazed at their lack of faith.

The centurion understood authority and had faith that amazed Jesus. The Jews in Jesus' hometown doubted the authority of Jesus; they thought they knew him well and, therefore, lacked faith (in spite of the evidence). There is a direct link between understanding the vast scope of Jesus' authority and our level of faith. If we really believe that he has authority over us, surely we will submit to him. If we believe that he commands the winds and the waves and that he loves us, we will ask him to still the winds and waves when our boat is capsizing on the lake. If we believe that he owns all the cattle on the hills, then we will ask him to slaughter only one to provide what is needed. Likewise, if we truly believe that it is neither power, nor influence, nor wealth that amazes Jesus, but faith—faith that moves mountains—that amazes him, then may we pray, as did the disciples, "Lord, increase my faith!"

Driving through the Intersection of Faith & Despair

EPHESIANS 1:5

I was preoccupied and never noticed the stop sign at the intersection and breezed through. My newly licensed teenager could not resist the temptation: "Uh, Mom, that was a stop sign and it applied to you." Jamming on the brakes, I stopped a hundred feet into the intersection (as if that would have done any good). My heart was racing in spite of the fact that there were no other cars coming; it had, thankfully, not been a near miss. I was nonplussed that I had completely failed to notice the intersection or the stop sign, which applied to me. Since then, I am twice as careful not only to stop at intersections, but to linger before entering (to the annoyance of my children). I look up the street, down the street, behind me, before me, beside me, determined never again to go through without paying attention to the stop signs. One never knows what might be coming.

I can tend to do the same thing in my spiritual life. I can go through the stop signs without noticing the intersection, until the Holy Spirit says to me (with less annoyance than my children): "Um, that was a stop sign, and it applied to you." These intersections, are, of course, as important, if not more so, than the physical intersection I cruised through.

The really significant intersections are where faith and despair meet. Sometimes, I have the wisdom to see that it is an intersection and I stop, looking in all four directions. At other times, unfortunately, I cruise through the intersection. Not until two or three hundred feet past the stop sign do I realize what should have been obvious: Not only was that an intersection, but it applied to me. That is typically a holy moment, which one might expect when faith and despair intersect.

Many years ago—certainly enough years that this story is told with the memory of, but not the actual pain—my husband and I struggled with secondary infertility. After the birth of our daughter, we were unable for the next four years to conceive again. After frequent visits to the doctor's office, we eventually decided it was time for a visit to the infertility expert. There had been too many cycles of hope and despair, too many cycles of expectation and disappointment, and not one cycle that had ended in pregnancy. We cycled through more disappointment as we waited for our appointment on October 10, 1997.

The night before my appointment, my husband kindly asked if I wanted him to go with me. Being woman, being strong, but not so invincible, I pooh-poohed the idea and told him he should go ahead to work. I could handle whatever the infertility doctor could throw my way. However, walking into the doctor's office I sensed I was in trouble. It may have been the rapid heartbeat or the tears forming just behind my eyeballs as I walked down the hallway, eyeing the happy pictures of success stories all along the walls. Somewhere along the forty-five-minute drive to this office, I had morphed from a hopeful and confident woman to a woman afraid and sad that our happy family picture would never grace the doctor's office walls.

The visit took all of half an hour. It seemed wrong that after we had waited and tried and hoped and prayed for four years, our future could be assessed in thirty minutes. The gentle, warm, and gracious smile I had envisioned giving me the solution to our four years of heartache was actually cold and matter of fact. "Well, I would recommend that you pursue adoption." No further tests necessary. No diagnosis. No smile. No gentleness. No reassuring hand on my shoulder. No further wisdom. The expert clearly had nothing to offer to salve my heart, let alone cure the infertility, so I left.

Through tears, I found my car and stood there, pounding on the hood of the car. *Where is Phil when I need him?* I was angry with my husband, angry with myself for telling him to go to work, angry with God that he was nowhere in sight, and I had not even told him to go to work! I leaned against the hood of the car, knowing I had no other choice but to continue to lean on the sovereignty of God. At the moment, I hated having nothing else to lean into; my trust and faith in him were more a Peter-like act of desperation than a joyful surrender. To whom else could I go?

Not long thereafter, we started the process of adoption, although we had a mere fifty-three cents to invest in the long and expensive process. We had already been told at the Cuyahoga County Children and Family Services Agency that the likelihood of our being successful candidates through the county adoption process was nil. Again, no warm, gentle understanding smile or explanation. And so we began the journey of international adoption.

We settled upon an adoption agency and started with the home study. When asked, our only country selection parameter was that it would not be Thailand. I had lived in Thailand for two years and had frequently heard couples staying at the guest house tell of waiting years for the adoption process, rife with obstacles and delays, to finalize.

In January 1998, Phil and I came to an intersection. We received a call and an email from two different people. Phil was checking the email on our third-floor computer, and I was in the kitchen checking phone messages. The phone message was from friends who had heard of our desire to adopt and wanted to fund the adoption, start to finish! The email was from a friend in Thailand who knew of twin boys needing an adoptive home. We each received these pieces of incredible news alone and ran to tell the other, meeting at the landing. Had we not come to the intersection of that offer of funding and children needing a home, I don't think we ever would have considered Thailand as a country from which to adopt. It was one of those intersections with a stop sign that we knew applied to us. We had to stop, take notice, look up, look down, look ahead, and behind. God was up to something. We could pursue this and ditch our original route with its parameter of avoiding Thailand, or we could stick to the original plan. We chose to recalibrate.

Again, we ran into disappointment. Tests run on the boys showed that one was HIV positive and the other twin was HIV negative. We did not want to separate the brothers. We could not fathom the heartache of our family to adopt a son and then lose him to AIDS. We brokenly said "No."

Where was God headed with this? Only a few weeks later, our friend emailed a request that we prayerfully consider another set of twin boys. Our prayerful consideration was short, but yielded an enthusiastic "Yes!"

Ten thousand miles past the intersection and eight months later, we flew to Thailand to pick up our sons from the orphanage. Few words can describe the intense wall of heat that greets a traveler stepping onto the tarmac in Bangkok. It didn't matter. The plane ride was an excruciating 27 hours. It didn't matter. The airplane food was, well, airplane food. It didn't matter. Our body clocks were 12 hours behind. It didn't matter. The adoption review board interviewed us with our entire life story spread out before them. It didn't matter. They approved us as an adoptive family. Two days later, October 10, 1998, we celebrated our sons' first birthday! We have celebrated many beautiful, thankful birthdays since then.

But I like to remember my sons' true birthday, the day they arrived into this world. It was the day that I leaned against the hood of the car, sobbing in the doctor's parking lot, feeling the pain of aloneness and hopelessness, wondering where the Lord was. How could I have known then, at that intersection of faith and despair, that he was indeed present and at work? At the moment I banged on the hood of my car, 10,000 miles away, on October 10, 1997, Thailand time, my God had already delivered my sons into the world.

Even now, years after I sailed through that intersection, I still slam on the brakes, my heart races and I marvel that, indeed, God is always at the intersection of faith and despair, and the stop sign applies to me, for I never know what's coming.

One More Thing

1 KINGS 17:7–16

Sometimes I feel like I cannot pick up one more thing to do. If my children ask me to take them one more place or arrange one more playtime, or if my husband asks me to get childcare for one more meeting, if one more person asks one more thing, I think I will erupt. The newspaper the next day will show black and white pictures of debris strewn all over Columbus, Ohio, with the headline banner sprawled across the Columbus Dispatch: "Mt. St. Ellen Blows Her Top."

I was having a day like that, begging the Lord to please spare me the one more thing. Of course, you know that as soon as you pray something like that, God may just show up with the one more thing.

He did it to the widow of Zarephath.

This amazing story made me laugh when I was in the middle of "Please, Lord, not one more thing." God told Elijah to go to Zarephath where the Lord had already provided a woman to give Elijah water. And sure enough, when Elijah got to the town gate, he met a woman gathering sticks. Elijah, remembering that God had promised he would provide a woman to give him water, boldly asked, "Would you bring me a little water in a jar so I may have a drink?" As she was going to get it, he called, "And bring me, please, a piece of bread."

Then the story gets really interesting. Being a godly man, Elijah advised her to go ahead and do what she had said (make a meal, eat it and die). But first, bring him some food.

Stop. Stop right there for just one minute. Can you imagine what this widow gathering sticks was thinking? If it had been me, I would have taken really good aim and thrown the very next stick at Elijah! The nerve! Not only does this man who doesn't know me from Eve ask me for water in the midst of a drought, he wants me to bring him some bread. I would have thought, *"Oh please, God, not one more thing."*

Without saying that directly, I bet she was thinking it. Doesn't it sound like there might have been a bit of an edge in her voice in her response to Elijah. "As surely as the Lord your God lives," she replied, "I don't have any bread—only a handful of flour in a jar and a little olive oil in a jug. I am gathering a few sticks to take home and make a meal for myself and my son, that we may eat it— and die" (1 Kings 17:12). Do you think this woman felt slightly overwhelmed and hopeless? She was at the end of her proverbial rope. She has no name. She is described only as "the widow at Zarephath." But I empathize with this woman. Drought. Hunger. No one to provide and care for her. The burden of caring for herself and her son is all on her. She's desperate. So desperate that she believes that gathering sticks for a fire to make a paltry meal will be her final act before she and her son die.

Along comes the prophet of God with an outrageous, outlandish, almost scandalous request: Get me something to eat. Not only that, when she declares, somewhat self-pity-ingly that she is about to prepare her own "last supper," it evokes neither pity, compassion, nor guilt in Elijah. Instead, Elijah says, "Don't be afraid. Go home and do as you have said. But first make a small loaf of bread for me from what you have and bring it to me, and then make something for yourself and your son" (1 Kings 17:13). Does that strike you as funny? It did me. In my abridged version: "Sure go ahead and die, but please make sure you have brought me my food first."

I don't know if that was the message God intended, but I laughed. That's what working in the church sometimes feels like. "I know, I know you've been doing children's ministry for 38 years, and you feel like one more month of children's ministry may kill you…but let's just try it and see if maybe it won't." Surely, you've been there! One more place to go. One more meeting to attend. One more errand to run. One more phone call to make. You feel dried up, sort of like that brook at Kerith Ravine. Someone has already come along and drunk the last drop. There just isn't any more. Then comes the request. It's outrageous. It's selfish! How could God bring one more thing into your life right now?

I don't know why the widow at Zarephath acceded to Elijah's request Maybe it was the custom. Maybe it was a rule of hospitality. Maybe it was tradition. But she did it, even though she was afraid. Elijah saw her fear and made her a promise. In spite of her fear, she believed his promise that the jar of oil would not run dry and the flour would not be used up. The widow at Zarephath went home, used up the last of her flour and oil, and made some bread for Elijah. When she did the one more thing, the miraculous occurred:

> So there was food every day for Elijah
> and for the woman and her family. For
> the jar of flour was not used up and the
> jug of oil did not run dry, in keeping with
> the word of the LORD spoken by Elijah
> (1 Kings 17:15b–16).

Sometimes doing exactly the one more thing we feel will kill us is the thing that brings us life. Sometimes committing to God's outrageously, scandalously huge opportunities brings us life when we would have chosen death.

What's your "one more thing?" Dare to believe, as the widow of Zarephath did,

that in giving and doing the "one more thing,"
your jar of oil will not run dry and your flour
will not run out.

Frogs and Fraud

EXODUS 7, 8

Satan is called many things in the Bible: the accuser of the brethren, a liar, a thief, a wolf in sheep's clothing, the devil, and a snake. None of those attributes is particularly flattering, and, well, they should not be. Today, I add to his already long list of titles: fraud. He is a fraud, a counterfeiter. Paul warns the church at Corinth, "... Satan himself masquerades as an angel of light" (2 Corinthians 11:14), but in the book of Exodus, the reality of the implication is quite evident.

It has to do with frogs. If you bring a frog into your home, and it hops like a frog, it looks like a frog, and is green like a frog, it's a frog. But if you say you can make millions of frogs come out of the water, up on the land, and they hop like frogs, are green like frogs, and look like frogs, but you cannot make them go back into the water, those green things may still be frogs, but you are a fraud.

A counterfeiter is a fraud who specializes in making and passing fake money. The counterfeiter works hard to make the counterfeit money as close to the authentic as possible. Counterfeiters try to use the same type of paper, the same ink, the same holograms and watermarks, and even embed the same fluorescent fibers in their "money." It doesn't have to pass as real money many times; it is enough for the fake money to pass as real only once to get the counterfeiter what he or she wants.

There were nine plagues before the sad and devastating grand finale, wherein every firstborn in the land of Egypt, save the firstborn of the people of Israel, was struck dead. The plagues were partly for Pharaoh, to give him an opportunity to repent from his idolatry (love of self), and partly for Moses to repent of his idolatry (fear of man). Mostly, the plagues were part of God's plan to set the people of Israel free to worship God.

Pharaoh was not about to let 600,000 slaves go without a reason, or at least a pretty good fight. On the backs of those slaves, Pharaoh had built the pyramids and the temples to himself. However, God wanted to set his people free, and if it required a plague and nine sequels to convince Pharaoh, so be it.

Therefore, God instructed Moses to take his staff in hand and perform miraculous signs with it (Exodus 4:17). The staff had a purpose: to prove to Moses that God was able to take that which was in his hand and perform miracles with it and through it.

The first time, Aaron threw his staff down in front of Pharaoh and his officials and the staff became a snake. Pharaoh's wise men and sorcerers did the same thing by their secret tricks; they threw down their staffs and the staffs slithered on the ground (Exodus 7:11). Pretty impressive! Except that "Aaron's staff swallowed up their staffs" (Exodus 7:12).

The second time, Moses raised his staff, struck the waters of the Nile and the water turned to a river of blood. The fish died, the river smelled and no one could drink the water. Those Egyptian magicians did the exact same thing (Exodus 7:20-22). Again, pretty impressive! Same miracle, but with a glaring exception: the magicians could not undo the miracle. Instead, the Egyptians used their brain power and dug along the Nile to get drinking water.

Third time was definitely the charm. This is when it became crystal clear that above the Hebrews' God there is no other, copycats and frauds below maybe, but no one like him.

But notice this one thing: the magicians and the wise men could not make the frogs go back into the Nile. The magicians were good at duplicating the miracle. But they could not undo what they had wrought by sorcery. Finally, Pharaoh could not ignore it. He could not out think it. He had to ask Moses, "Pray to the LORD to take the frogs away from me and my people, and I will let your people go to offer sacrifices to the LORD" (Exodus 8:8).

The third time and every time after that, the magicians, the sorcerers, and the wise men could not undo the fraud. They ignored the consequences of their actions, working around them, but they flat out could not undo them.

Like the magicians and the wise men, we cannot undo the consequences when we try to reproduce the works and miracles of God. We seek pleasures for the sake of pleasure and so crash and burn in alcohol or drugs. We find our meaning in success and find there really is nothing at the top of the ladder. We seek identity apart from God and end up finding identity by trying to be someone other than who we were created to be. We try to live without God at all and find that self at the center of the world is ultimately scary and lonely. Whatever puny pleasure-seeking act it is, if we try to mimic God's actions out of our flesh rather than according to the word and power of God alone, our snakes will be swallowed up, our water will remain bloody, and the frogs will remain in our bedrooms, on our beds, and in our ovens and kneading troughs.

In our own ways, we, also, can be frauds, relying on our flesh, on our brains, to counterfeit the gifts and miracles of God. Those counterfeits may pass as real once, maybe twice, but the truth remains, it is only counterfeit. Eventually, we must deal with our counterfeits.

Excuse me—I need to go take a good close look at my bedroom, my oven, and my kneading trough!

Missing Marcia

Marcia is missing.

Marcia is my sweet, older sister who mentored me in being a sister, being a mom, and homeschooling my children. She taught me pretty much anything I know about being kind and being gentle. If you know me and wonder where those qualities are, believe me, the fault lies with the student, not with the teacher.

She started going missing about three years ago. She would ask me the same question three or four times within an hour. I was not irritated; it is hard to be irritated with Marcia. It was just odd that she was asking me the same thing. Of course, if you ask my children, I myself am on repeat mode with some of my questions. But that isn't what I mean either, and that is a different essay.

Marcia got me into scrapbooking. When Marcia first started scrapbooking and selling scrapbooking products, she approached it in that unassuming Marcia sort of way that made me want to buy from her. We would spend hours cropping our pictures. While she spent hours designing her pages, I just slapped mine into the book on a piece of pretty mounting paper. I didn't care about the scrapbooking. I just loved being with Marcia. I would purchase my scrapbooking stuff, spending way more than I needed to. At the end of our session, she would add it all up, figuring out the tax, because she is meticulous in that way, while I gagged as I emptied my wallet. Smiling, Marcia would say, "Someday when we are old and sitting in our rocking chairs, looking at these albums, laughing hysterically, you will thank me." Like so many other times, she was right, of course.

On this particular day, when Marcia's illness was made clear to me, we were at my kitchen table with years' worth of pictures laid out before each one of us. Marcia held up a picture of a field trip to the zoo that she, her five children, and I with my (then) three children had gone on together. She stretched her arm out across the piles of memories on the table, smiling her beautiful smile, and asked, "Hey, do you remember when we all went to the zoo this time? Look at how cute the kids were." She handed the picture to me and when I saw how geeky we looked, I laughed. I knew if my children ever saw that picture they would never forgive me for letting them out in public dressed like "that." We chitchatted about that field trip and I handed the picture back to her, resuming my very intense scrapbooking. My intensity was broken when, not five minutes later, she held up the same picture, tilting her head in her Marcia way, and grinning that same beautiful Marcia smile, asking me, "Hey, do you remember when we went to the zoo together?" I let it pass, answering her with the same two-or-three sentence conversation we had just had. In that moment, it struck me as a little strange, nothing more.

Later, we sipped tea. Marcia likes only herbal tea; she is a bit of a health nut. She very tentatively mentioned that she was a little worried, concerned, that she was starting to lose her short-term memory. Again, the comment struck me as odd, but this time I did not let it pass.

"Really? How so?"

"I don't know. Just little things. I think I ask people the same things two or three times, but they don't say anything. I don't remember things on the schedule, even though I write them down. I ask the kids several times where they are going. Other people don't say anything but the kids tell me all the time; they get annoyed. That's how I know."

I could not let it pass, not this time. Marcia was looking for me to validate that it wasn't just her imagination, so I circumvented. "Well, Marsh, I forget things too."

I then did what I always do when I am un-comfortable: I talk. I have to be intentional about stopping. I was getting really uncom-fortable. So I talked. I told her about every little thing I had forgotten in the last week, wanting to make her feel better, hoping to make her forgetfulness go away, even though I knew my forgetfulness was not the same as hers, nor would her forgetfulness go away. But I desperately wanted it to. Fortunately, or unfortunately, as it turned out, I stopped myself and asked her the question none of the siblings dared to articulate.

"So, do you think it might be Alzhei-mer's, like Opa?" Opa, our grandfather, had been diagnosed with early-onset Alzheimer's when he was around age 55, and I remember it very clearly. I hated his Alzheimer's. I can't remember exactly how old he was when he was diagnosed. When you are eleven, it doesn't matter and anyone over twenty-five is ancient. Sitting across from me was my fifty-seven-year-old sister. She was not ancient. It did matter. She was Marcia and I wanted her to not have Alzheimer's.

I guess asking the question was what unlocked the emotion, because Marcia started to cry, in that I-don't-want-to-be-a-bother way that Marcia has.

"Maybe. But the neurologist says he does not see anything."

I stumbled around looking for tissues to hand her. "Well, that's a good sign, isn't it? We are getting older Marcia. We all forget things." Marcia answered me in very not-Marcia fashion: she said to me very firmly, very clearly, "No, because I know I am forgetting things. And if he does not see anything, he will not do anything." We drank our tea and finished scrapbooking.

That day, when she added up my habit's financial damage, Marcia quietly and apologetically said, "I know I need to figure out the tax on this, but I am not quite sure how to work the calculator." I helped her figure out the tax. Marcia got on the road back home where she could not remember whether she had salted the dinner or not. I stayed at my kitchen table and sobbed uncontrollably. Marcia is missing, and I miss her.

The Accidental Explorer

DANIEL 3; PSALM 12:5-6

The children still talk about it, and I can even laugh about it now after many years. When we first moved to Columbus, we went on a hunt for the local library. My husband had given me "sort of" directions but had accidentally forgotten the second half of a two-name street. Not ever seeing the two-name street, I never turned and ended up looking for the library in an industrial park about ten miles away, two hours, many wrong turns, and much frustration later. How many times can you listen to, "Hey, Mom, I think we already passed this, but it was on the other side of the street before?" As it turns out, the library is six minutes and four turns from our house. I had spent a lot of time driving in circles and every other conceivable geometric design, going very far to get to a place that was very near.

However, after months—years—of driving in circles, getting lost, and generally gorging myself on MapQuest® and Google® maps, I am getting to know my way around. In fact, sometimes I'll be driving down a street intersecting another and think, *This looks vaguely familiar. Oh, I didn't know this street connected with this.* Or, *Wow, I had no idea that these two roads ever met. Hey, I didn't know I could get here from there.* It comes from years of driving in the same neighborhoods and, frankly, being willing to get lost on the road and driving until I get to where I need to be. Getting lost is never fun, but accidental exploration of familiar territory is exciting, for me, anyway.

Likewise, although I have been reading the Bible for decades, sometimes I think, *Hey, this sounds familiar, but it was on the other side of the page the last time. Or, Hmm, does this scripture connect with this other one over here?*

This is how it happens. Pretend you are in the car with me, reading scripture together. Drive straight to Psalm 12:5-6:

> Because the poor are plundered and the
> needy groan, I will now arise," says the
> LORD. "I will protect them from those
> who malign them." And the words of the
> LORD are flawless, like silver purified in
> a crucible, like gold refined seven times.

Note the signs: furnace of clay…purified seven times…protected from those who malign them.

Now a soft left turn into Daniel 3. This is the account of three young men who feared God in a foreign land more than they honored the king. King Nebuchadnezzar, the head of the Persian Empire around 600 B.C., had built a rather ostentatious statue to himself. Further, he had set up a handy schedule by which everyone in the empire would know the proper time to turn, face the statue, fall down, and worship it.

But there were some Jews in the kingdom, namely Shadrach, Meshach and Abednego who neither served Nebuchadnezzar's gods nor worshiped the image of gold he had set up. Nebuchadnezzar's wise men saw this as a perfect opportunity to get rid of their rivals (Daniel 3:12). The other jealous wise men ratted on these three young captive leaders, who were brought before King Nebuchadnezzar to account for their refusal to bow to the statue. He demanded that they bow like all the other good subjects of the kingdom, or he would throw them into a very hot furnace. They were willing to suffer the consequences of their faith in God. They refused to bow down trusting that God could save them from the furnace, but even if he didn't, they would not bow down to Nebuchadnezzar (Daniel 3:16-18).

Stay with me, I'm still driving, but no longer in circles. I am seeing familiar signs. My turns are a little less random.

Nebuchadnezzar was furious. He ordered the furnace heated SEVEN TIMES HOTTER than usual. Hey, this scripture intersects with Psalm 12:6! The very high, "seven times hotter than usual" heat, that Nebuchadnezzar intended to incinerate the young men to ashes was the same heat that God intended to purify these young men, as silver is refined seven times!

Take a hard right here, because I think I am on to something.

Why does Nebuchadnezzar order the furnace to be heated up seven times hotter than normal? Wouldn't the fire have burned up these young men in their "robes, trousers, turbans and other clothes" anyway? Nebuchadnezzar heated up the furnace so hot "that the flames of the fire killed the soldiers who took up Shadrach, Meshach and Abednego" (Daniel 3:22). The fire, seven times hotter than normal, was intended by Nebuchadnezzar to incinerate the men completely. God intended it to purify them, like silver in a furnace of clay, intended that they would come forth as a testimony of his grace, power, and protection, without even the smell of fire on them. And when they came out of the furnace Nebuchadnezzar praised the God of the three young Hebrews. He commended them for being willing to defy the King's order, and were willing to give up their lives rather than serve or worship idols or Nebuchadnezzar (Daniel 3:28-29).

Do you feel like you're in a furnace right now? Is it getting hot? Consider this possibility: the flawless word of the Lord is written on your heart, like silver purified seven times. You are also his letter known and read by everybody. You show that you are a letter from Christ "written not with ink but with the Spirit of the living God, not on tablets of stone but on tablets of human hearts" (2 Corinthians 3:2-3). You are his word, his letter, refined in a furnace of clay, stoked seven times hotter than normal. So also will you be purified seven times, for the display of his splendor. Was that too many left turns?

My Glorious Humble Calling

EZEKIEL 9

My first writer's conference was a challenge. It wasn't the speakers. It wasn't the schedule. It was not the material presented. It wasn't even the cost. The mental struggle every time I thought about actually attending a writer's conference caused me to hyperventilate. *I am a fraud. I am not a writer. Who am I kidding? I should not be going to a writer's conference. Writer's conferences are for writers.*

The challenge was packing, getting into the car and standing at the registration desk of the Indiana Faith and Writing Conference (IFWC). The conference definitely provided fodder for thinking, processing, articulating ideas, and, hopefully, writing. However, like most professional conferences, IFWC also gave opportunity for consultation with published authors, editors, and publishers.

Writing consultants, as in any profession, give good news and bad news. Every time I gingerly, apologetically, slid an essay across a table to be reviewed, I lied, "Yes, I want honest feedback." What I received then was, of course, honest feedback. This is good, this is not so good. This is effective. Hmmm...this is weak. Yet, for all the honest feedback, which, I concede, was wanted (sort of), needed, and appreciated, I left the coaching sessions challenged, excited, somewhat offended *(What? You don't think it is perfect?),* wondering whether I was called to write. Regardless of my mix of emotional responses, at least I acquired a new arsenal of tools for my writing tool kit.

The day after I returned from the conference, the challenge, wonder, and excitement of the conference still churning inside me, I met the man with a writing kit at his side (Ezekiel 9:2).

"Perfect," I thought. *"He can help me wade through my mix of thoughts and fears."* Believe it or not, a nameless, ancient man with a writing kit at his side helped me process all my takeaways from the conference!

About 2600 years ago, the prophet Ezekiel had a vision of Jerusalem. In the vision, Ezekiel also saw "Six men...each with a deadly weapon in his hand (Ezekiel 9:2). What snagged my second look as I read this portion of Ezekiel was the description of the man in linen. He had a writing kit at his side. He too must have just attended a writing conference. What did the man in linen write that would merit him a mention in the most popular, most read, loved, and maligned book ever written? I knew I could learn from him. And, since I had just filled my own writing kit with new tools; I was ready to be taught. I learned quite a bit from the man in linen.

Writing is a calling. The man in linen hung out with six men armed with dangerous weapons. The man in linen had no dangerous weapon. He had a writing kit. Of course, he knew the pen is mightier than the sword. He was not called to be a guard by the altar or a bodyguard or a fighter; he was not called to do the task of the six men armed with dangerous weapons. But he was called. "The Lord called to the man clothed in linen who had the writing kit at his side and said to him, 'Go'" (Ezekiel 9:3).

Writing assignments can be very humble. The man was dressed in linen. He was equipped with state-of-the-art writing implements. He was ready for the assignment, writing kit at his side. His assignment? "Go throughout the city of Jerusalem and put a mark on the foreheads of those who grieve and lament over all the detestable things that are done in it" (Ezekiel 9:4). Surely not, Lord. A mark? Wouldn't a letter be better? A five-paragraph essay perhaps? At least one or two pithy sentences? A mark? Okay, a mark.

Humble writing assignments can be deceptively profound and critical. The mark that the man in linen wrote throughout the city of Jerusalem protected those who bore his writing. "Slaughter old men, young men and maidens, women and children, but do not touch anyone who has the mark" (Ezekiel 9:6)."

Obedience to the call is its own success. "Then the man in linen with the writing kit at his side brought back word, saying, 'I have done as you commanded'" (Ezekiel 9:11).

Do I write? Yes. Am I writing all I have been commanded? The answer to that question is still waiting to be answered. For now, it is enough that I am clothed in linen and have a writing kit at my side, ready to hear, mark, and obey.

Waiting for Redemption

LUKE 15: 11-32

The story of the prodigal son is famous. Rembrandt painted a picture of it. Henri Nouwen wrote a book on it. Songs have been written about it. It is the story about a son who went to his father and demanded his inheritance. The father gave the inheritance, even though it was not the right time for the son to get that inheritance. And, of course, the son squandered it. Some pastors say that the story is more about the kind and compassionate father, the merciful father who welcomed back the prodigal son with open arms and great rejoicing. Then the story becomes one in which the father is a picture of God who, even when we literally spit in his face, forgives us when we return. When I listen to such a sermon, I am very thankful that I have such a kind and loving father in heaven. It is a good and right interpretation of the parable.

However, this is a parable. In parables, the symbolism isn't quite as tight as it is in allegories. Knowing that, I allow my mind to wonder a little bit about the father in the story. Let's assume that the father in the story is not a type of God. Let's assume he is a picture of a human being, a father who demonstrates incredible love and mercy, yes, but a human father, nonetheless. Well, as a human father, he is not perfect. And therein lies the seed of today's essay.

I wonder about what happened before

the son left. I wonder whether the father and son fought for months and years before the father relented and said, "Yes, here is your share of the inheritance." Did he argue with his son? Did he try to convince him to pursue another course of action? Were there weeks of tension in the house? Did people walk around on eggshells for fear that the wrong Hebrew word might be spoken? Was it a miserable time for the family? Did the son sulk around the house, slamming doors? Was the older son gleeful at the thought of his younger brother leaving, as he had threatened?

Sometimes I wonder how long that father waited for the younger son to return. Was it a matter of months? Was it years? Was it a matter of days? Did the father go through a period of thinking, *He'll be back soon enough!*

Then he'll see. Then, did the father move to, *What if he never comes back?* or *Surely, he's got to come back!*

Here is my biggest wonder: Did he ever sit there on the doorstep thinking, *What did I do wrong? How did I get to this place with my beloved son?* Maybe he even played the litany in his head: *Was I too strict? Was I too easy? Was I stubborn? Was I too controlling? What could I have done differently? How could I let him go? God of Abraham, Isaac and Jacob, what if he never comes back?*

I think many parents go through that period, the waiting for the redemption of a pain. For some, it is not a big pain. For some, the pain is excruciating. Some pains in raising children can be so deep and chronic, we wonder if "the wound is incurable" (Jeremiah

30:12).

Families go through the pain of children who leave under less than storybook circumstances. Not all, but many. And they grapple with the issue of how long before redemption comes. *How long will I wait for my wound to heal? Will I ever be whole again? Can I ever be whole again? Will I ever be able to not hurt? Will my child ever forgive me? Will this nagging ache ever go away?* For some, it isn't a long wait. For others, it is a dreadfully long wait. Some go through it thinking, *Ha! They'll see what life is like out there in the cold harsh world. A little reality check is all he or she needs to come running back.*

After thinking about the prodigal's father as a human parent—an imperfect parent, a parent like me or like my husband—I concluded that the father of the prodigal son could have thought all those things. He could have thought every single one of them. He could have done the litany in his head a thousand times, if he did it once. But what I love is that even if he did recite the litany of the shoulda, coulda, woulda's, he did not stop going out to the porch. He didn't stop looking. He didn't give up hope. He did not accept the present as the forever. He stationed himself daily on the doorstep—watching, hoping, looking, and scanning the horizon, waiting for redemption.

And one day, there he was. A tiny dot in the far distance. How could he not recognize that lanky gait? Surely it was his son. And off the father ran.

I am on my doorstep waiting for redemption. Are you? Are you waiting for the redemption of a pain? A wound? Do you think your wound is incurable? Too deep? Too wide? Your fault? Do you go through the litany? As a believer, I do not wait for understanding, for figuring out the why and the why not. Ultimately, I wait for redemption from the hand of the King. So, I am waiting, but I look and I scan, and I do this in confidence: "Since ancient times no one has heard, no ear has perceived, no eye has seen any God besides you, who acts on behalf of those who wait for Him" (Isaiah 64:4). Beloved friends, I am not waiting for the situation to change, although I do believe it may; I am not waiting for anyone to change, myself included. This, too, shall surely happen. I am not waiting for anything or anyone other than the Lord himself. I am waiting for him, for he himself is my redemption in any situation, any circumstance, any pain, and any wound.

God is a God of redemption. Will he who redeemed the cross withhold any other good thing from us (Romans 8:32)? If you, too, are waiting for redemption, remember that our God is in the business of redeeming. Therefore, keep hoping, keep looking, keep scanning the horizon, keep waiting for him who is our redemption. "Surely, God is good to Israel; those who put their trust in him will never be disappointed" (Isaiah 49:23).

Lessons on the Ladder

JOSHUA 23:8

Our last house had cedar shingles. So when we moved to a newer house with vinyl siding, I was delighted. Of course, there is still the wood trim. Right now we are in the throes of painting the trim, which requires a lot of time, lots of paint, hours of scraping, and of course, the big, megaserious extension ladder. I intensely dislike standing on a sloping roof, and although I am not a great fan of heights, I can paint on an extension ladder. I can, but I am not very comfortable doing it. Don't look down. Don't. Look. Down!

One hot, humid, summer day, there I

was—perhaps twenty-five feet up—painting the very highest peak on the house. I take each rung one at a time. One foot on. The next foot on. I cannot bound up the ladder as I do the stairs. The ladder shakes. Painting up there—twenty-five feet closer to the outdoor temperature of ninety-four degrees—I am pressed into the ladder so hard that the imprint of each rung is on my legs. I find it very difficult to let go of the ladder. Holding onto at least one side at all times makes painting very cumbersome and time consuming. And, I just cannot stretch as far when I am gripping one side of the ladder.

About the third day of doing this—this clinging and hanging on for dear life—it occurred to me that clinging to the ladder probably does not make me any safer. The safety issue is pretty much determined as I, or my husband, set up the ladder on level ground, test it, bang it against the house a few times, and decide that the ladder is stable. The steadiness and sureness of my position is not in any way linked to my clinging to the ladder. The steadiness and sureness is in the setup of, and in, the ladder itself. I can be clinging hard to the ladder as it falls to the ground if the ladder isn't steady and on level ground! For sure, I feel better when I am clinging hard to that one side. I somehow feel that I am safer or that I am more secure if I am hanging on.

Perhaps your child has clung to you during a thunderstorm, head burrowed into your shoulder, arms wrapped so tightly around your neck it is suffocating. Your child's eyes are screwed shut until the storm is past. The fact is, you are holding onto your child. It is the parent holding the child, but the child is hanging on, clinging to the parent, for dear life. It does little good to say, "There, there, you don't need to choke me." The child needs to do so, until the storm is past. I suspect my children, too, felt better, safer, and more secure in hanging on so tightly, in clinging to us during the storm. No amount of reason, rationale, or logic could persuade them to let go. They needed not only to know the storm would pass, they also needed to feel safe and secure until the storm was past.

Sometimes, I just need to feel safe in the Lord. I know I am. I preach to others, and to myself, we are safe in the Lord. But, oh sometimes, I so need to feel that safety. And God is patient. Even though I am hugging him so hard his divine face might turn blue, he won't let me go or try to give me logic and reason in place of safety and security. He lets me cling so hard to him that I wear the very imprint of his face on mine. I feel his arms around me, tightly holding me, and I cling to his neck.

By the fifth day of painting, I could actually climb up to that peak, look down, and think, "Wow, I'm pretty high," and then I would let go and hold two brushes or the paint can, if necessary. It was amazing to me. I still disliked climbing up a high ladder, but I could do it, all the way up, whistling all the way. Not that I was confident in myself. I found my confidence in the ladder and the level ground on which it rested. I knew, even if I let go of the ladder, it was still bearing me.

Beloved, if you're on a faith ladder right now, "hold fast to the LORD your God" (Joshua 23:8). Know that the ladder is secure, strong, and will not fail you. The ladder, if resting on Jesus, is on a sure and steady foundation. If you feel better clinging to the ladder, if you feel safer holding on tightly, rest assured he doesn't mind. Besides, the tighter you cling to him, the more you will bear the imprint of his face on yours.

Not bad for a summer lesson on the ladder.

Unconventional Weapons

EPHESIANS 6:12

History is replete with unconventional weapons: mustard gas in World War I, the atom bomb in World War II, napalm in Vietnam. In this age of weapons of mass destruction, it is, at best, disconcerting to read of dictators in faraway countries flexing their nuclear muscles for the world to see and tremble. And so countries sit in their respective corners, fingers on the buttons, secret codes memorized and distributed to the trusted few, waiting for some insult—real or imagined—that the buttons may be pressed. The presidency of George W. Bush was marred by arguments as to whether or not Iraq really had weapons of mass destruction. Recently, the media was rife with reports of Syria's use of chemical warfare against its own people. We, as Christians, are engaged in a great spiritual struggle. In our journey as believers, are we to take up such weapons of mass destruction?

The Bible is very clear that "our struggle is not against flesh and blood, but against the rulers, against the authorities, against the powers of this dark world and against the spiritual forces of evil in the heavenly realms" (Ephesians 6:12). We have an unconventional enemy who is, at times, unseen. Although we may see the powers of this dark world, we may not see the spiritual forces of evil in the heavenly realms. Yet both exist. And certainly, as Christians, we would be wise to see and to acknowledge the effect and the toll of both in our world and take up arms. But what arms? What weapons?

Most who have walked shoulder to shoulder with others in the fellowship of faith have frequently heard the instructional verses that describe the weapons of our unconventional warfare. We don the belt of truth, the helmet of salvation, the breastplate of righteousness, and the shoes of the Gospel of peace. Additionally, we take up the shield of faith, and we wield the sword of the Spirit (Ephesians 6:13-18).

However, in discourses on those precious verses, we are always reminded that the only offensive weapons in the arsenal are the sword of the Spirit and prayer. I do not intend to diminish the strength of the armor nor the power of the offensive weapons. My purpose today is to reflect on the weaponry in our personal arsenals. "What weapons?" you ask.

> For though we live in the world, we do not wage war as the world does. The weapons we fight with are not the weapons of the world. On the contrary, they have divine power to demolish strongholds (2 Corinthians 10:3–4).

The weapons we fight with are not the weapons of this world. Here is a less than awe inspiring and fear inducing inventory of weapons taken from the annals of biblical history:

A staff. A jawbone, Torches. Jars. Trumpets. A slingshot.

Moses had a stutter and a staff. He was unimpressed with the staff he used in his daily shepherding. Yet, we know the things that happened as he wielded the staff: snakes slithered, gnats annoyed, frogs hopped into Pharaoh's bed, and the waters of the Red Sea were parted.

Samson found a "fresh jawbone of a donkey" and struck down a thousand Philistines (Judges 15:15). I have tried, many times, to envision this. I can't. It is just too odd!

Gideon had an even less impressive weapon—jars with torches inside. God allowed Gideon only three hundred men to fight against all the Midianites, Amalekites, and other eastern peoples who camped in the Valley of Jezreel (Judges 6:33). Although it seemed like the numbers were stacked against Gideon and the three hundred Israelites, "[T]hey blew their trumpets and broke the jars that were in their hands" (Judges 7:19-20).

God seems to delight in confounding the world, and us, with his use of such strange and unconventional weapons in the hands of equally unconventional leaders, judges, and warriors. Ordinary people. Ordinary people, like myself, who ask, "How can I be an effective agent of change for the kingdom of God in the years I have remaining, in a world and culture that desperately need him, yet daily deny and resist him? How can I war against, not flesh and blood, but against the powers of this dark world and against the spiritual forces in heavenly realms? And with what weapons?" That burdensome question, once again.

I take up my pen and all that my pen represents: my prayers to God, his answers

back to me, his story, my story, journal en-
tries, Bible studies, and reflections on my
culture, letters never finished, letters never
sent, writings born from floundering and
from faith. My pen is a weapon, albeit not
of this world. It is my jawbone, my staff, my
sling, my stones, my jars, and my trumpet.
God willing, and by his power, it will demolish strongholds. What unconventional weapon do you hold?

The Stroke Trilogy

It never crossed my mind that one of my parents would have a stroke. But then, as a sinful human being, I just thought the ill happenings and afflictions of life would fall on others, preferably the unjust. Although I give intellectual assent to King Solomon's wisdom that it rains upon the just and the unjust and time and circumstances overtake us all, it was not until the summer of 2012 that circumstances overtook my family. A stroke befell my precious father. The things I have observed and felt through the dual life lenses of affliction and faith have turned my intellectual assent to an emphatic "Amen!"

Part I: Seamless Love

We've heard of all kinds of love. Timeless love—love that makes time stand still. Endless love—love without end. Puppy love—love that is immature. One summer I learned of a different kind of love: seamless love. Seamless love—love without seams.

In July, 2012, my father suffered a cerebral hemorrhagic stroke. It left him immobile on his right side and unable to communicate well. That is an understatement. Since the stroke, he has had two bad infections, one of which nearly killed him. It has been a journey for all of us, most particularly my father and mother. The stroke happened three weeks after they celebrated their sixtieth anniversary.

Theirs was a story of young love. After several years in Japanese and Indonesian concentration camps during World War II, they were married in Jakarta. She was 19, and he was 21. They moved to the Netherlands and then to America with their young family. My parents suffered much discrimination as immigrants to America, yet managed to become quite successful. There are probably few couples who could match either one of them in their fervent love and loyalty to one another. But that is not what seamless love is.

I witnessed seamless love in the rehabilitation center, where my father stayed after the stroke. My mother and I waited 45 minutes for an aide to come help my father after he had had a bowel movement. My father, still incapacitated, was unable to walk or stand. My mother pressed the button for the nurse to come. We waited, but no one came. I went out to the nurse's station and explained my father needed help. No one came. No one came. And no one came. My father was uncomfortable; he was getting agitated in his discomfort. I was uncomfortable as well, but for different reasons. It was an odd feeling to know that my father, who seemed to rule my world when I was little, now could not control his bladder or bowels. My mother, on the other hand, is not one to bother with feelings of discomfort. So she did what she always does. She did it herself. The cleaning, I mean.

She didn't need help from an aide and she didn't want help from me, which was probably a good thing. She walked over to the bed, and then very gently and tenderly started talking to my father, explaining that she was going to clean him and, clucking her tongue, chided the aides for not coming. All the while that she was talking to him, she rolled him on his side so she could remove the filthy diaper. Gently, ever so gently, she pulled down his sweatpants, took off his diaper. Never, not once, did I detect one hint of resentment or disgust.

I watched in disbelief, and a thousand thoughts went through my head.

Oh my goodness, it smells! That's my father. This is her husband. My father wears a diaper now. This is her lover. This is her life companion. She's cleaning his bottom. She's using wipes. This is weird. This is beautiful. This is humbling. This is humiliating.

And, all the while, my mother was whispering, laughing with him, talking gently to him to make sure that he was neither uncomfortable, nor embarrassed. In about 10 minutes, she was finished.

Then, without skipping a beat, she leaned over, nuzzled him and whispered, "Hey, I miss sleeping with you at night. You need to get better and come home. I miss you." It was as if I was not even in the room. I could not hold back tears as I witnessed such beauty, humility, and intimacy. I felt like an intruder. To witness such a moment of intimacy is an honor. And humbling.

In that moment, I understood seamless love. It is the seamless movement from the dirt and filth of reality and life into the wonder, delight, and intimacy of true and genuine love. It is a woman who is able to clean her lover's bottom and love him and whisper her aching and longing for him. It is the seamless movement of a father lifting up his robes, running down the road to embrace his pig-slopped son. It is a God who takes us out of the pit of our disgusting filthy sin, picks us up into His divine arms and holds us close in redemptive love and grace. That is seamless love.

My Mental
Labyrinth

2 CORINTHIANS 10:5

If the skull protects the brain, what protects the mind?

The brain is, understatedly, an amazing organ. I hadn't thought much about it until a few years ago, when three separate tragedies befell our family: in the same year my father, at eight-three, had a stroke, my brother-in-law, at forty-nine, had two strokes, and my sister, at fifty-eight, was diagnosed with early-onset Alzheimer's. Each of them had brain-altering events that affected their lives.

When my father had his stroke, I responded in the way I typically and most comfortably did: I read. I read books on strokes, on the brain, and how to help someone recover from stroke. I engaged in the same mental exercise when my brother-in-law had his strokes. And I did the same thing when Marcia was diagnosed with early-onset Alzheimer's. I learned about the brain with its flexibility and its rigidity. The brain is confounding. It opens our lives to broad and expansive horizons, thanks to its capacity to learn, reveal, and interpret. Yet it closes our lives to the two claustrophobic choices of fight or flight.

The mind, too, is awesome. It is different from the brain. We know this because we say someone is losing their mind, not their brain. Maybe it is the difference between one's body and one's identity or the difference between one's humanity and one's soul. I have been considering this a lot lately, because there is a labyrinth in my mind through which I sometimes wander. Turning the corners and facing the next barrier is simultaneously fascinating and scary.

I had an episode in the mental labyrinth today. On my way to the gym, I reached for my iPhone® armband in the glove compartment, and could not find it. I always put the armband in the same place: the glove compartment. Not finding it in its place, I immediately started to panic. Not because I could not buy another holder. Not because I did not know where it was. I panicked because I could not remember if I had put it in the glove compartment. My reaction probably seems disproportionate to the temporary loss.

However, because Alzheimer's disease stalks my family generationally, I am more and more careful to follow routines. My keys go in a certain place when I come home. My phone goes to the same location as often as possible. My purse hangs on the same kitchen chair. I write down a menu each week. I write my passwords in a secret book that I put in a secret place; I dread the day the location of the secret book is a secret to me. None of these details and rituals is earth shattering. But I know Alzheimer's could affect my brain, so my mind is determined to fend off the disease or, at least, its effects, with these little steps. Therefore, when I misstep, when I misplace an appropriate word or my iPhone armband, I get unreasonably frustrated.

When I could not locate the armband, I immediately said something to my husband. I started to sweat, my heart pounded, and my mind raced—not my brain, my mind. I immediately went from *Where did I put the armband?* to *This is a sure sign of early-onset Alzheimer's.* In less than one minute, I had gone from a functioning 58-year-old woman able to remember, research, investigate complex cases and fact patterns for work, and multitask a graduation party, a birthday party, a family vacation, to a woman who was completely unable to think through, or past, where she had put her phone armband. I was certain that I was another step down the road toward dementia.

Fifteen minutes later, I was in the gym, doing my weenie weights workout, but I was calm and thinking appropriately. However, I was still in the labyrinth. I was running through the possible realities. The scientific reality is that early-onset Alzheimer's can be generational. My grandfather and two uncles had Alzheimer's. And now my sister.

The everyday reality is that I function well. I still work and am managing a household effectively, if not to everyone's liking, I care for my parents and can plan events. The once-in-a-while reality is that I misplace some mundane, necessary object and I spend twenty minutes looking for it. I forget a password that I use frequently, and I have to change it (again). I cannot remember the appropriate word to use and fumble through my mental dictionary, sure that I know the word is there, if only I can remember it. And then, I have an inordinate, disproportionate response to the misplacing or the forgetting. All the while, as I run through the labyrinth, I am desperately thinking:

Am I just stressed out?

Am I forgetting in the same way the way my other friends, who are also 58, forget things?

Am I forgetting and misplacing things more than my friends?

Am I forgetting and misplacing in the way Marcia did and we did not see anything, or saw, but did not say anything, for fear of the ugly possibility?

If I am thinking through all these issues, can I even have Alzheimer's?

As I was desperately stumbling through the matrix, I said to myself again and again, "I have the mind of Christ. I have the mind of

Christ." I quoted Scripture to myself to fend off the lion that prowls about seeking to devour my mind and overtake my brain with fear and anxiety: "You will keep [her] in perfect peace, whose mind is stayed on You, because [s]he trusts in You" (Isaiah 26:3 NKJV).

I talked with my husband. He reassured me he saw no signs of any unusual memory lapses, promising that if he did, he would tell me and we would walk through it. I called a friend who promised she would tell me. Then, on a practical level, she advised me to keep track of the episodes and talk to a doctor. All good advice and all sweet assurance.

Some weeks ago, Marcia came to visit with me in my home for a few days. It was fun and "normal" until she looked at me and asked me whose house we were in and whether it was my house. I held it together just long enough to excuse myself, go to the bathroom, and have a cry. Alzheimer's is awful. Marcia, sometimes tearfully, but always determinedly, presses into as much of life as her failing brain cells allow.

Sometimes, Marcia comes to church with me, and she takes notes, as she always has, but now with spelling errors, words crossed out as she realizes the spelling isn't quite right but unable to figure out what is wrong. Her brain isn't what it used to be. But when Marcia sings a worship song, she lifts her hands to the Lord in love and worship, I see that she is kept in perfect peace as her mind is stayed on him. Her mind is focused on him and his unfailing love for her. For a moment, she is a picture of centered peace in the midst of a labyrinth.

All that reading after my father's stroke taught me that my skull protects my brain. My faith and the Word teach me that the Lord protects my mind as it is today and as it one day might be. I have the mind of Christ and he will keep me in perfect peace, as my mind is unalterably, unwaveringly, stayed on him. With that, I get out of the labyrinth, take a deep breath and "demolish arguments and every pretension that sets itself up against the knowledge of God, and I take captive every thought to make it obedient to Christ" (2 Corinthians 10:5). I have the mind of Christ, and that keeps, and will keep me, on a path of peace.

Gawking at the Sky

ACTS 1:10-11(A)

> They were looking intently up into the
> sky as he was going, when suddenly two
> men dressed in white stood beside them.
> "Men of Galilee," they said, "why do you
> stand here looking into the sky?" (Acts
> 1:10-11(a)).

Well, why do you think? Jesus had just

given them the most significant, challenging,

important, and life-altering job assignment

they would ever receive. He was talking

about power, the Holy Spirit, witnessing in

Samaria and Judea ... and suddenly, he was

gone. Whoosh. Like a David Copperfield

magic act, Jesus was gone. Was he coming

back? When would he appear again? What

were the disciples supposed to do next? Wait? Leave? What? For the disciples, Jesus' sudden disappearance was just another strange event in the series of strange events of the past two months.

When Jesus triumphantly entered Jerusalem I can just imagine the disciples somewhat smugly thinking, gleefully, *Woohoo, we are in good with this extremely popular guy who is going to rule Israel and conquer the Romans!*

Then, Jesus gets arrested and dies on the cross and the disciples might have thought, *Oh no. We don't really want to be seen with this guy.*

Three days later, the really weird happens and Jesus rises from the dead. By now, the disciples must have been really confused, thinking *Having a hard time with this.*

For the next forty days, Jesus appears now here, then there, sometimes to one, sometimes to all, leaving the disciples wondering, *Are you staying, or not?*

Here they were, after the forty days. Jesus and the disciples were having a conversation. The disciples were thinking about power and ruling over the Romans, the restoration of a kingdom. They wanted to know times and dates. They wanted everything to happen now. Jesus patiently answers.

> It is not for you to know the times or dates the Father has set by his own authority. But you will receive power when the Holy Spirit comes on you; and you will be my witnesses in Jerusalem, and in all Judea and Samaria, and to the ends of the earth (Acts 1:7-8).

The spirits of the disciples must have sagged as Jesus said this. Imagine what was going through their minds. Jesus was talking about power from the Holy Spirit and being his witnesses. He told them they were going to go into Samaria. Samaria? What was that about? No one even walked through Samaria! They had always been taught to walk around Samaria. Then, to make matters more complicated and confusing, Jesus told them they would go to the ends of the earth, wherever that was. And how long would it take for them to walk there? They needed to know, because, as far as they understood, once they had gone to the ends of the earth, he would restore the kingdom of Israel. And now, before he could tell them just how far it was to the end of the earth, suddenly he was somewhere else.

Why wouldn't they be staring intently at the sky? Picture the disciples, heads up, gawking up at the sky into which Jesus had disappeared, mouths hanging open, completely undignified!

Some years ago, my husband and I felt called by God to start a new ministry, necessitating our leaving a very safe and comfortable job. We had four children, one of whom was about to be launched to university, a home with a mortgage, and the typical daily needs, like eating, for instance. We have held jobs such as project manager, lawyer, and pastor. Now God was calling us to something totally different. This was the biggest assignment of our lives. There was the rush of the excitement of the new calling, the fears of leaving the familiar, the pain of change and transition, the joy of confirmation in the call from

Jesus. Then, suddenly, he was gone! A cloud hid him from what we could see. Confusion flooded in. What? Jesus, where are you? Was that you? Did you really say these things to us? If so, then where are you now?

Beloved, have you ever felt like Jesus was hidden from your sight by a cloud? Maybe when you went through a painful situation? Perhaps you got laid off from the job for which you moved across three states and yanked your children out of school. Perhaps you were betrayed by your spouse. A myriad of circumstances left you feeling confused, bewildered, angry, disappointed, just plain lonely, or even abandoned.

About two months into the new thing, I was staring intently at the sky, as if staring at the sky would force Jesus to appear, hold my hand, and assure me all was well. As if looking at the sky with intensity and anticipation would force his hand. I wasn't waiting for his instruction; it was his presence that I wanted. Then the Lord, in that wonderful still, small voice of His, reminded me of one truth: "I am with you. I'm in the cloud."

> By day the LORD went ahead of them in a pillar of cloud to guide them on their way and by night in a pillar of fire to give them light, so that they could travel by day or night. Neither the pillar of cloud by day nor the pillar of fire by night left its place in front of the people (Exodus 13:21-22).

Regardless of our feelings of abandonment, of desperate aloneness, of confusion, or bewilderment, God is present. "The LORD himself goes before you and will be with you; he will never leave you nor forsake you. Do not be afraid; do not be discouraged"

(Deuteronomy 31:8). He will never leave us, but sometimes he may be hidden by the cloud. The very cloud that hides him from our feeble, fleshly eyes is the cloud wherein he dwells. Don't despise the cloud. Don't curse the cloud that hides him from your view. The cloud is actually the sign of his presence with you. Follow the last instruction he gave. Remember his promise to never leave you, and don't just stand there, gawking at the sky.

The Stroke Trilogy

Part II: Save the Last Dance for Me

My parents have danced since forever. I don't mean the teenage hanging-on-to-each-other that too often passes for dancing. I mean the real deal. Fred Astaire and Ginger Rogers gliding across the room, waltzing, fox-trotting, and rumba-ing, tripping-the-light-fantastic kind of dancing. At our Dutch–Indonesian community gatherings in Boston, they danced. At New Year's Eve parties, they waltzed to Patty Page singing "Tennessee Waltz." At Christmastime, as soon as I heard the strains of "Silver Bells," I knew they would soon be box stepping out of the kitchen, and my father would grab my mother and dance her into the living room. When they got really wild, they would do a tame version of Chubby Checker's Twist. They danced. They loved it, and they were good!

At times, when we were younger, my siblings and I would shoehorn ourselves between them. As we got older, they would rope us, their five children, into dancing as well. They never taught us, other than by example, but we somehow managed to stumble our awkward teenage feet across the same dance floor they were tearing up. I can recall cha-cha-ing with my brother. You may think that was gross, but it was fun.

When my parents got older, they discovered ballroom dance clubs; so they joined one. Every month, my father would put a tuxedo on his very distinguished frame and my mother would get into her dancing dress (often, one she had made), and they would join their friends on various dance floors across Cleveland.

As I mentioned, they never really taught any of us to dance, and frankly, they were such great dancers—so adept, so smooth, and so elegant—it became less fun to watch them, let alone to dance with them. It was too intimidating. Many people would comment on how graceful, how perfectly in step they always were. And they were. Sometimes, my father would oblige the rules of formal dancing and dance with another woman, but you could tell he was most comfortable dancing with his bride.

To my parents, dancing was not merely fun; it was an art form. My mother would often correct one of us in our adolescent attempts to dance with our father. She even corrected my father's missteps! Sometimes, they would practice at home, and I could hear my mother scold my father for a misstep or a mistake in the rumba rhythm. But even so, it was always impressive to watch them. Like watching Olympic skaters, I could admire them and enjoy the show, but knew I could never aspire to it.

One of my fondest memories will always be my father asking me to dance at my parents' fiftieth wedding anniversary party. Previously, I dreaded these moments, because I knew I was not a fluid dancer like my mother and he may have felt compelled to lead a little too forcefully, overcorrecting my awkwardness and lack of grace. And, I feared, he may have felt a little obliged to dance with his daughter! But this night it was different. The joy of fifty years with his bride, having all his children and grandchildren around him, and the delight of dancing had put him into a gracious mood. He put out his hand for me, I accepted and he led me onto the dance floor. I, of course, immediately apologized for not ever having learned to dance and he simply said, "Relax, I will lead, you just have to follow." And suddenly, with my father, then seventy-four, and I at forty-five, it really didn't matter whether I got every step right or danced as well as my beautiful, graceful, perfectly stepping mother. It was fun; it was a moment of delightful intimacy with my father.

Even into their seventies, my parents were still dancing—at their clubs, at home on Christmas, and at new configurations of the Dutch–Indonesian Society—wherever they had a chance. In fact, my mother still was buying dancing shoes at age seventy-nine. She had just bought a beautiful pair of silver ballroom dancing shoes to match a dress she had purchased for a dancing date already on the calendar when my father had the massive stroke that debilitated him severely.

I drove her home after his first day at the hospital, an exhausting, frightening day that began early that morning, with the first signs of something terribly wrong. We left him in his hospital bed unable to speak or move, tubes running in and out of his body, unable even to call for the nurse. My mother was drained. As we walked into the kitchen, there on the counter was the box of silver dancing shoes, still waiting for the dance, two eternal weeks away. My mother, ever practical, glanced at them, stifled a cry and simply remarked, "Well, maybe I should go ahead and return them. I will not need them anymore." I tried to encourage her, "Mam, keep them. You never know what can happen."

Seven months later, my mother stunned me by announcing that she and my father were going to Florida and they would be fine. If someone could take them to the airport, they would be met by two attendants pushing two wheelchairs at the airport. She had even rented a car. I think she thought this foresight and planning would reassure me. I was not reassured; I was terrified. How would they manage? What if he fell? His gait was so unsteady, so unsure, and so awkward when he shuffled through the house. How would they manage a wheelchair at the hotel? What if something happened? Well, of course, something did happen.

I called her Valentine's Day night, still a little irked that she had taken this risky trip, and asked how she and her Valentine had celebrated. "Ellen, you will never believe what we did. We danced! We danced. The hotel had a Valentine's Day dance, and Papa and I danced. Oh, it was wonderful! Of course, he missed some steps (she laughed), and he could not turn me the way he used to, but we danced. It was perfect."

And so this beautiful couple ballroom-danced their way out of graceful, perfectly timed and executed steps and into the perfect delight of simply being able to dance together. Such is the perfection of the divine dance as well. Not the accomplishment of perfectly executed steps, but simply delighting to dance with the Lord of the dance.

A Dog's Tale

For years, our children begged us to add a dog to the mix of our already busy family. Finally, when our twin sons were eleven years old, we relented and welcomed Gabby to our family. When we picked her out at the animal shelter, Gabby was still a puppy, untrained, mischievous, and always hungry. About three weeks after we brought her home, that puppy energy and our busy family life collided.

Before we left to spend the evening at the local zoo, I planned ahead and put a twelve-quart pot of beef vegetable soup on the stove, out of Gabby's reach, on the back burner. Everything went according to plan, as we came home, ate dinner, and the boys headed upstairs to get ready for bed.

The situation went south, however, when I was interrupted from cleanup detail by two boys needing to be tucked into bed. Without thinking to put the soup back to its proper location on the back of the stove, I answered the summons. But no sooner had I entered their room, when the three of us heard a loud crash and an unmistakable yelp!

We arrived on the scene to see Gabby, standing in the middle of the kitchen floor, lapping up beef vegetable soup as quickly as she could. There was soup everywhere, on the cabinets, under the refrigerator, some had already spread to the living room carpet. It was a nightmare.

To make matters worse, I instinctively scolded the dog, which caused her to lie down in the soup. My follow-up rebuke led to the next mishap, as she stood back up and shook her entire body, flinging soup into every conceivable nook and cranny that hadn't already been tainted by the initial spill.

Since the entire mess was really their fault (they had asked for the dog, right?), I yelled at my sons, "Go straight upstairs to bed!" Paul pitifully asked, "Mama, you aren't going to send Gabby back, are you? I'll help clean up the mess, Mama. Don't send her back." One withering look from his frustrated mother was all Paul needed to dutifully trot off to bed. Instantly, I felt terrible.

And so, in the wake of this disaster, I found myself gingerly navigating my way through a soggy bog of soup and upstairs to my boys' room to apologize to them, reassuring them of my love and care for them. At the same time, I had to ease their concerns about Gabby, who they now assumed, was on her way back to the shelter. I said, "Boys, you need to know that Gabby is part of our family now, and just because she does naughty things, it doesn't mean we are going to send her back. Things don't work that way when you're a family."

I was totally unprepared for my sons' reactions. Sam reminded me that I'd signed a contract with the animal shelter, so of course I wouldn't take Gabby back. True enough, I supposed. But Paul nearly broke my heart when he piggy-backed on Sam's appeal: "Yeah, just like you signed a contract with the adoption agency in Thailand and promised you would take care of us and keep us even when we do naughty things."

In that moment, I was struck with just how sad and pathetic it would be if all that held us together was some kind of paper-and-ink contract signed many years before. Still trying to take all this in, I answered, "Boys, a contract is not what makes us a family. Love makes us a family, God's love, and the fact that God has chosen us for one another." I wanted to convey a sense of security and a sense of belonging, even a sense of uniqueness, in having been chosen and adopted that far out-weighed any sin or imperfection. "Our family is not a family because Papa and Mama signed a piece of paper. We are a family because God chose us for one another and we love each other."

And isn't that what our Heavenly Father has been trying to teach us all along? His acceptance of us, His children by faith in Christ, is based on His love and His love alone. Just like my love for my children, God's choice of us is no mere contract or impersonal paperwork. It's deep and personal to the point where "the Word became flesh and dwelt among us."

By taking on flesh, dwelling with us, dying in our place and defeating death for us, Jesus identifies with us in such a deep, personal way that Hebrews 2:11 says, "He is not ashamed to call us brothers." In other words, we're family, and since we are, we have no need to appeal to contracts, paperwork, or performance.

Our status as God's family, his sons and daughters, is infinitely secure because it's based on the love of the God who always makes good on his promises. This faithful God is the God who is eternal, infinite, all-powerful, and extravagantly near.

Each one of our children, three adopted and one birth child, was placed into our family by God Himself, and we are constantly affirming each one with the words, "You are ours. God has chosen you for us and us for you." In the same way, I hear my Heavenly Father say, "You are mine. Nothing changes that. I have chosen you. I have adopted you as my daughter, and I love you. Even when you spill the soup."

When Curiosity Did Not Kill the Cat

EXODUS 3:1-10

"Curiosity killed the cat" is actually a curious expression. For years I parroted this idiom to my young children as the temptations of electrical outlets, hot stoves, power tools, and valuable treasures in high places beckoned to them. As they got to be middle-schoolers, they would frequently hear one or two words of a hushed conversation with my husband and interrupt, "What, what, what does that mean? What are you saying?" It would aggravate me and I would throw out the idle threat, "Curiosity killed the cat." It had the desired effect. Perhaps too much so. Now I want them to be more curious! As they have gotten older, I want them to ask questions and to want to know about the world around them, particularly because their world's borders are limited to what their two thumbs can reach on a smart phone.

The truth is, curiosity does not always kill the cat. In fact, curiosity sometimes can bring great reward to a cat. What would have happened had Moses not had just a modicum of curiosity?

Moses had just spent approximately the last forty years in Midian, tending sheep in the midst of pagans, far from the country of his birth, and far from the country of his divinely promised inheritance. He was separated from his own people. There in the desert, he had a lot of time to think. A lot of time to think about things he would not do again, like get into the middle of two fighting people. Who knows if he thought about the God of Amram and Jochebed, his parents? Did he think about the God of Abraham, Isaac, and Jacob? He was on the far side of the wilderness and there he came to Horeb, the mountain of God.

That part of the landscape is particularly barren. A bush, in and of itself, would have been sufficient to qualify as a strange site. Now throw in the fact that the bush was on fire. Either Moses never heard the expression "curiosity killed the cat," he had heard it but chose to ignore it, or he saw something bigger than his curiosity. "Moses saw that though the bush was on fire it did not burn up. So Moses thought, 'I will go over and see this strange sight—why the bush does not burn up'" (Exodus 3:2-3). It was a strange site. He threw caution and care to the wind and went over to examine it.

There, in the midst of his curiosity, the Lord appeared to him. "When the LORD saw that he had gone over to look, God called to him from within the bush, 'Moses! Moses!'" (Exodus 3:4). Moses had to respond to the strange and curious site before God called to him. Sometimes, all it takes is recognizing that something is slightly unusual to nudge us into response. How often we read in the Bible about someone who noticed something different or odd and the result is an encounter with God Himself, Jacob had a dream at

Bethel of angels running up and down a ladder. "When Jacob awoke from his sleep, he thought, 'Surely the LORD is in this place, and I was not aware of it'" (Genesis 28:16).

When Joseph was in prison and saw his fellow inmates looking dejected, he asked them "'Why do you look so sad today?' 'We both had dreams,' they answered, 'but there is no one to interpret them.' Then Joseph said to them, 'Do not interpretations belong to God? Tell me your dreams'" (Genesis 40:6-9).

The centurion who oversaw the crucifixion of Jesus, "seeing what had happened, praised God and said, 'Surely this was a righteous man'" (Luke 23:47).

The disciples walked around Jerusalem doing good deeds, including healing a lame man. People wondered at what they observed in the disciples: "When they saw the courage of Peter and John and realized that they were unschooled, ordinary men, they were astonished and they took note that these men had been with Jesus" (Acts 4:13).

I sometimes wonder how many encounters with God himself I have missed because I was too lazy to go over and see. How many divine appointments have I lost simply because I was too consumed with the mundane activity associated with tending my sheep? Or, how often have I been so overwhelmed by the barrenness of a wilderness that I just didn't even think that the presence of the Lord might actually be there?

The Lord was in the burning bush and from within the bush, God called to Moses and spoke to him something even stranger than a burning bush: "So now go. I am sending you to Pharaoh to bring my people the Israelites out of Egypt" (Exodus 3:10). How could Moses know that if he went to Egypt, he would see God do even more amazing things-even more amazing and curious than a burning bush.

The Stroke Trilogy

Part III: Communion

Since my father's stroke, my parents have not attended church very often, although my father does enjoy attending church. Church attendance has been part of his life, especially singing hymns. He loves hymns, and although he could not always remember the words well, he liked to whistle the tunes. When my father was in the hospital and then in the rehabilitation center, my sister and I made it a practice to sing hymns with him before saying good night. It seemed to soothe him; it made the involuntary jerking of his hand stop. There was something beautiful and profound to hear him singing along in monosyllabic guttural sounds because he cannot speak very well anymore. I cried as my sister and I sang "How Great Thou Art," and he sang along with "ahhhh." I cannot imagine God enjoying a sweeter sound in heaven.

This particular weekend, our family went to visit my parents and took them to their church—a smallish, white clapboard-sided Episcopal church called St. Christopher's by the River—complete with a liturgy and priest in white robes and a stole. Because the Episcopal Church follows a lectionary, a series of readings appointed for each day, the priest delivered a sermon on the baptism of Jesus. Then we celebrated communion, which is a ritual wherein the priest takes the host (the wafer) and the wine (real wine) and blesses it, saying the appropriate, accompanying prayers. In Episcopal tradition, the priest literally feeds the congregation, in remembrance of Jesus' last Passover with His disciples.

I have participated in this ceremony hundreds, if not thousands, of times, having been raised in the Episcopal Church through my early twenties. It is a beautiful ceremony, tainted by familiarity. I was neither moved nor comforted by the ceremony.

The preceding week had been emotionally wrenching. I had reflected on the series of losses for our family. I had cried many tears. I felt raw. I heard the priest say, quoting from The Book of Common Prayer, "This is my body, which was broken for you; do this in remembrance of me. This is my blood, which was shed for you, as often as you shall drink; do this in remembrance of me." I was hearing, but not really listening. The priest then turned to the congregation and invited us to come to the altar rail, kneel, and receive communion. I went up dutifully and frankly, thoughtlessly, still reeling from the events of the past year. I returned to the pew to wrestle with my questions and the pain of others' afflictions. I heard the continued murmuring of the priest, "This is my body, which was broken for you..."

When everyone who wanted to receive the elements (the wafer and the wine) had gone up, the ushers separated a part of the rail, leaving an opening for the priest. At that moment, the priest picked up the chalice of wine and the plate for the host, faced and scanned the congregation. He walked from behind the altar, past the communion rail and straight to my father, where he stopped. Then, he invited my father to participate in the holiest of moments for a Christian.

I was touched as the priest tried, for what seemed like several minutes, to place the wafer into my father's shaking hand. He held the body of Christ this way, he held it that way, but my father could not seem to take hold of it with his right hand. The priest then picked up the wafer and placed it directly into my father's mouth, "Jerry, this is Christ's body, which was broken for you; do this in remembrance of Him."

He continued. "Jerry, this is Christ's blood which was shed for you; do this in remembrance of Him." Because of his very unsteady hands, my father could not tilt the chalice toward his mouth and there was a bit of messy sloshing of the wine. It didn't matter. They tried again, and this time, my father was able to tilt the cup to his mouth, with help from the priest, in remembrance of Jesus.

That was when I started to cry. How much are we all like my father in the presence of God's holiness and sacrifice? We cannot manage to take hold of the presence or holiness of God. Therefore, Jesus stands in the gap and does what we cannot do in our flesh; he brings the presence of God to us in his flesh.

I had not expected to find Jesus in the traditional ritual of communion. But isn't that exactly where I should have expected to find Jesus? I saw Jesus in the priest, coming from behind a communion rail, stepping down into the nave, walking down the aisle to meet an 83-year-old elderly, shaky man, who often stumbles, often hesitates. I saw him stand before my father, allowing him the dignity and the humility to participate in communion with God and with his church community, by giving him the body and blood of Jesus. He invited my broken father to share in a celebration that is for all the broken, all the sad, all the weary, all the sinful.

That is the role of the church and the community in which God has placed us. I too, must get out from behind the altar, walk through the openings in the communion rails at which I kneel, look out and find the ones who cannot walk—the broken, the hurting, the lonely, and the sinful. I must bring them the body and blood of Jesus, by being the body of Jesus, so they too might celebrate with me in remembrance that Christ died for them and for me. Amen and amen.

Coming in
at 601, 730

NUMBERS 26:51

I ran one marathon. I did not intend it to be my only marathon, but it has been, so far. I have also run several half-marathons and some 10-K runs. Regardless of the length, the races are always packed. Typically, the fastest runners are put at the front of the pack. The rest of us unworthy mortals are spread throughout the herd according to our self-estimated speed. The goal, cruel and undemocratic as it sounds, is to let the fastest ones run unhindered, without being slowed down by the rest of us 10- or 15-minute milers. My one marathon was quite an experience, from standing around waiting for the instruction to go, all the way to reaching the finish line.

Standing there, waiting for the gun to go off, I feel like a 4-minute miler. I know I'm not, but for some reason I feel I can run faster than I actually do. It is probably adrenaline. Or I am just delusional, or it is the power of being with the superior runners, spurring me on. Regardless, there I stand, elbow to elbow with people to the left, right, before, behind, and all headed for the same place. If I am far enough back in the pack, as I always am, I can barely see the starting line, let alone the finish line. All I wait for is the firing of the starter gun. And once it goes off, everyone takes off—slowly! Way in the back of the pack, I can barely move my feet.

The great thing is that at the end, people on the sidelines were still cheering the slowpokes along. They stood along the route and cheered. In my case, it was enough to give me that extra kick. Somehow, although hundreds, if not thousands, had already finished and crossed the line, it did not matter that I was not first or second or even last. I had crossed the finish line alive. My first goal was to cross. My second goal was to cross on my feet versus in an ambulance. Mission accomplished!

In Numbers 26:51, it says that there were 601,730 Israelite men, twenty years old or older, who were able to serve in Israel's army. That means those who were not able to serve in the army, perhaps because of age or some disability, the women, and everyone under age were not counted. So the total number of people who crossed the Red Sea and who were rescued from Egypt was, well, a lot. Some commentators say, more than a million.

Many times, I have tried to picture that crossing in my head. The Red Sea, at the historically accepted point of crossing, is about 400 meters wide—that would be about 1,312 feet. What I try to envision is one million eager people, moms holding children, husbands frantically pulling families, people trying to help the aged and infirm get across, hearing the sound of Egyptian army chariots, horses behind them all the while, and water, walls of water, on either side.

Picture a million or more people at a crossing point 1,312 feet wide. One million Israelites did not link arms and stroll across the Red Sea as one long surge. Nope. I am about twenty inches wide. (Don't try to picture that, just accept it, please). It does not take a math genius to know that twenty inches × even 1,000,000 people is a lot of inches, more than 1,312 feet. I suspect the situation resembled a marathon. There were probably four-minute milers, some ten-minute milers, and probably a whole bunch of twenty-minute milers.

Imagine being the ten-minute miler in that crowd of more than one million, all the way at the back of the pack. You can barely see Moses. *Where is that guy anyway? For that matter where are Miriam and Aaron? I should have stayed in Egypt.* Right about this time, you may be thinking, *Am I going to make it?* If you are a ten-minute miler, let alone, a twenty-minute miler, you can almost feel the hot breath of Pharaoh's chariot horses behind you. All you want is to cross the sea and get to the other side, to safety.

"[T]he Israelites went through the sea on dry ground, with a wall of water on their right and on their left" (Exodus 14:29). And so, every single last one of them crossed to safety—the weak, the strong, the women, the old, the young, the infirm, the infants, plus 601,730 counted Israelite men. And the walls of water did not sweep back over the Red Sea until number 601,730 crossed the finish line. As soon as number 601,730 crossed the line, the race was over. "The water flowed back and covered the chariots and horsemen—the entire army of Pharaoh that had followed the Israelites into the sea. Not one of them survived" (Exodus 14:28). Every single one of the Israelites finished the race! And if you are a ten-minute miler, like I am, that brings a sense of relief, gratitude, and victory. Welcome to the finish line!

The Worth of Wisdom

1 KINGS 4:29-34; 1 KINGS 11:9-11

Solomon is known as one of the smartest and wisest men in the world who ever lived. Yet, for all his wisdom and writing about getting wisdom and living wisely, he was not wise enough to place a premium on wisdom in his own life and follow his own words of wisdom.

Maybe you know the story: God appeared to Solomon, the son of David, the King of Israel, and gave Solomon an incredible invitation: "Ask for whatever you want me to give you" (1 Kings 3:5). Rather than asking for wealth, victory over his enemies, long life, or any other thing for which ordinary folk might ask, Solomon asked the Lord for wisdom. "So give your servant a discerning heart to govern your people and to distinguish between right and wrong. For who is able to govern this great people of yours?" (1 Kings 3:9). God saw Solomon's humble, responsible, and zealous heart. Solomon was humble enough to recognize there was no way he had the requisite wisdom to lead God's people. He had a sense of responsibility to lead God's people in God's ways. He possessed a zeal for God and for God's renown. God saw Solomon's humble, responsible, and zealous heart. In fact, it so blessed the heart of the Lord when Solomon asked for wisdom, that God gave Solomon not only wisdom, but wealth, honor, and a long life.

God answered Solomon's prayer in spades! God gave Solomon wisdom, insight and understanding beyond measure. His wisdom was so great that his fame spread to all surrounding nations. "The whole world sought audience with Solomon to hear the wisdom God had put in his heart" (1 Kings 10:24). God gave Solomon an extraordinary platform for proclaiming the greatness of the God of Israel to the world. Solomon received an incredible opportunity, one that had never been given to anyone previously, and perhaps, not since.

How is it, then, that the wisest man in all the world did the dumbest and most foolish things—things that led to his personal demise, his family's failure, and the fall of his kingdom? How did he fall so far from God, from grace, tumbling from that wonderful platform?

"King Solomon, however, loved many foreign women besides Pharaoh's daughter–" (1 Kings 11:1). Solomon had been warned as an Israelite and as a king to stay away from foreign women, not to intermarry with them, "because they will surely turn your heart after their gods. 'Nevertheless, Solomon held fast to his seven hundred wives of royal birth, and three hundred concubines" (1 Kings 11:3). Solomon's wives and concubines turned his heart after their gods. He built temples for Molech, for Chemosh, for Ashtoreth, and for every single one of the gods of every single one of his wives.

Solomon had wisdom, yet because he lacked self-control, he lost his kingdom and peace in the land; his own sons rebelled against him. But was it just for lack of self-control? Solomon himself wrote, "The fear of the Lord is the beginning of wisdom" (Proverbs 9:10).

It was by more than disobedience in the area of marriage, adultery, and intermarriage with pagan wives that Solomon squandered his platform. Solomon stopped fearing the Lord. Had he feared the Lord, he would have obeyed the very thing that God said to him, not once, but twice.

> Although he had forbidden Solomon to follow other gods, Solomon did not keep the LORD's command. So the LORD said to Solomon, "Since this is your attitude and you have not kept my covenant and my decrees, which I commanded you, I will most certainly tear the kingdom away from you and give it to one of your subordinates" (1 Kings 11:9-11).

Is this tragic irony? That the man who had wisdom from God to write that "wisdom begins with fearing God," stopped fearing God, gave in to his selfish, base instincts, and lost a kingdom? It is grievous to see someone who starts so well, finish so poorly.

Perhaps my greatest life lesson from one of the smartest men in the world is to walk in the fear of the Lord all my days, so that at the end of my days, I do not forsake the Lord and his Word and so lose the platform, however small or expansive, God has given me to speak of his glory in the earth.

Loving Quietly

JAMES 1:17

I live. I mother. I wife. I lawyer. I daughter. I sister, and I friend. All those non-verbs—all those things that I am—demand that I do. So I cook, clean, love, make love, talk, cry, help, read, analyze, marvel, think, process, make decisions, raise teenagers, cry some more, kiss my husband, laugh, and dance with my children. The list could go on touching most every verb in the dictionary from Aa to Zz.

My life is far from quiet. It is a continual melding of activities and blending of significant and peripheral peoples' lives into mine and mine into theirs. But several months ago, my life was pushed into a period of reflection simply because many markers had suddenly appeared on my life's road. Suddenly, not as in "unexpectedly." Suddenly, as in, "Wow, am I already this far along on the journey?"

For instance, my husband and I had just celebrated 24 years of married bliss. We talked about our first date, first kiss, and first night. Our daughter had gone back for another year of college, fraught with all the tension that the process of finding and form-ing identity brings. Our twin sons turned 19. It was easy to think back to holding them at the Chiang Mai airport for the first time, face to face. Our second daughter was thinking through college choices and mapping her fu-ture career. My father had a stroke, and this very intelligent man, who spoke at least three languages fluently, was telling my sister, "My hand is a fox." My mother was learning to live a new normal after sixty years of intimate and day-to-day conversations with her husband, who now struggled to communicate. My routine now consisted of regular drives from Columbus to Cleveland with many monotonous miles of highway on which to think and reflect.

My Father in heaven has often been, and is now, very quiet in his love for me. He is often not flashy in the ways he demonstrates love for me. I thought about this when my daughter mentioned something about a gift she had been given and asked me if I remembered any conversations that would have set the giving of the gift in motion. Ah, my maternal pride would have loved to say "Yes, I was totally behind it." But as I could not honestly say that, I simply admitted, "Sometimes the Lord is just quiet in the ways He loves us." Sometimes, he leaves no calling card, no gift card other than the gift itself. And he leaves it up to us to trace the gift to the Giver.

Why? Why not have flash and bang and sis-boom-bah when he leaves the gift? A little gift card that unabashedly and incontrovertibly announces To: Ellen, Love: God. It makes things so much easier at bridal showers, for instance, when someone sits beside the bride-to-be and carefully keeps track of who gave what. That way no giver will feel unappreciated or unloved. In fact, nowadays, givers receive note card envelopes pre-stamped with the soon-to-be bride's return address, on which the giver writes her address, making sending thank-you notes easy for the bride-to-be. Why doesn't God make it that easy and just leave his pre-stamped, self-addressed calling card or gift card along with every gift? Why risk being unappreciated and unloved, and why not get acknowledged?

I think it is because gift cards mandate "Thank me." But, when our precious Father in heaven quietly leaves a gift, it says, "Seek me." We start the process of tracing the gift to the Giver and, coming face to face, we can say to him, "Thank you. I didn't realize it was you. But now I see."

I know that "Every good and perfect gift is from above, coming down from the Father of the heavenly lights…" (James 1:17). But sometimes, amid the verbs and doing, I forget that thanking Him does not always lead to seeking him, but seeking him and finding him as the giver of every good and perfect gift does lead to thanking him.

The Snake in My Hand

EXODUS 3

Picture a little man sitting cross-legged in front of a basket, playing a flute. As he plays, a snake, usually a cobra, slowly uncoils out of the basket, swaying back and forth to the beautiful music to the amazement of the crowd surrounding the man. Then, slowly, deliberately, the little man continues his song and the snake winds itself neatly back into the basket.

That's a lot more impressive than a man picking up what he thinks is a stick only to find that it is a snake. That man will scream, throw it down, and run away as fast and as far as he can. Welcome to Exodus 3.

What's with the staff and snake thing in Exodus?

Some years ago, Phil and I noticed that the face boards over the garage were peeling. We ignored it. We wanted it to get really ugly before we did anything. We would mention it to each other and promptly do nothing. One spring, as I moseyed up the driveway, I again noticed the peeling paint and knew that we needed to do something. Ignoring it was not making it go away. So, I went to the local paint store and bought some paint with a name too log and grand for its purposes.

Of course, as soon as I got home, I didn't like the paint color. So the paint sat and the face boards and trim on the house continued to peel and look bad. For two weeks I was paralyzed with the fear of putting that paint on our house and not liking it. What if everyone in the neighborhood also hated the color? What if our daughter, who is very color conscious and design savvy, also hated the color? Would she be too embarrassed to invite her friends home? What if my husband's boss saw it and fired Phil over the color of our garage and trim paint? You can see why the color I had chosen kept me awake at night.

As I walked in our neighborhood, I noticed the successful color prowess of everyone else in the development. I was amazed at how well everyone else could select the perfect colors to enhance the beauty and value of their home. So, I prayed for a color-selection anointing. You may be shocked to learn that

I did not receive it! Instead, I heard in my head, *What is that in your hand?*

I was a little stunned, taken aback by the question, because I knew that God knew what was not in my hand. I did not have the right paint.

"Uh, I have a paintbrush and a gallon of customized paint that I cannot return and which cost me $34."

Just use it. You will never find the perfect color unless the name is perfect-color-for-face-boards-over-the-garage-and-trim. Just use it.

So I did. I used the paint I had bought, and guess what? I really like the paint color and although I have visited the same unmentioned paint store probably twenty-five times since then, I haven't felt the strong urge to repaint the house. My husband was not fired over the color of our house, our daughter has even invited friends over to our house, and no one in the neighborhood moved because of my butternut-colored paint.

What's the lesson I learned? Use what is in your hand.

Although he did not know the extent of it, Moses was on the cusp of the biggest assignment of his life. He had an idea that it was big, bigger than he, otherwise he would not have argued so much with the Lord. Through the burning bush, Moses got the invitation to approach the living God. Then he heard the voice of God Himself say "I love my people, I have heard their cry, I remember my promises to them, and I'm here to answer their cry. Now you go." Moses tracked with God all the way up to "now you go." But the more God talked about the people, the king of Egypt, the bondage, the king of Egypt, 400 years of slavery, the king of Egypt, the weight of the covenant, and the king of Egypt, the more Moses began to realize that he was getting enmeshed with the plans and purposes of the God of the universe, and it was scary. "They won't believe me or even listen to me," he objected.

God's response to Moses is very interesting. He essentially discounted Moses' credibility, persuasive powers or fluid speech. Then, God asked Moses, knowing all along what the answer was, "What is that in your hand?" To his credit, Moses does not give the eleven-year-old-boy answer, "Nothing." "'A staff,' he replied" (Exodus 4:2). Of course, it is a staff! Moses is a shepherd. He was out doing his shepherding thing. He was out minding his own business, doing what he had chosen to do in Midian, a thing he was doing well, when suddenly he saw a burning bush. The thing in his hand was the tool of his trade.

Then comes the part we learned about in Sunday school: the staff turned into a snake. The tool that guarded and calmed sheep became a thing that sheep feared. It was scary enough that Moses himself ran from the snake. And probably everyone else would run away from it as well. At God's command, an ordinary tool of our trade can become something fearsome to those who might oppose us.

Then the snake became a staff again. God told Moses to grab it by the tail and it reverted to a harmless, but effective, useful tool again.

Do I know that when I follow the Lord's instructions, the tool in my hand may become something fearsome but controlled?

I am a writer and a talker. I have a friend who, when asked, "What's your gifting" sometimes answers, "I talk!" Then, she laughs her wonderful laugh and elaborates on her answer. The truth is, talking is her gifting. It is also my gifting. I talk and I teach, following the maxim, "The pen is mightier than the sword." The tools of my trade are my tongue and now, the computer keyboard. I speak and I write.

But oh, how often those very same tools become my worst liabilities! I say things I cannot pull back. I write things and hit "send" before I have cooled off. I speak the words that stay forever in cyberspace. Sad as it is, the maxim holds true—the pen, the keyboard, and the tongue are mightier than the sword, sometimes causing greater pain than the point of a rapier. The staff in my hand becomes a snake. And then, like Moses, I want to run away from the very gift God has given me.

Yet, the truth cannot be ignored: the thing in my hand is often the very thing that God wants me to use to tackle what could be the toughest assignment of my life.

What is that in your hand? Is it a color you don't like? Maybe it is something you are second-guessing. Maybe it is something that you don't think is very cool or sexy or necessary or important. Maybe it is something way too familiar. But what is in your hand?

Are you using it? Rather, are you letting God use it? Or is that "snake" just sitting in the basket?

Don't wait for the select-the-perfect-color anointing. Hear the Lord; obey the word of the Lord, and watch for him to perform his word.

May I Borrow Your House?

MARK 2:1-12

I love to host people. Lots of people. When I host, I like things to be, well, perfect! I can imagine how I would have responded had I been the host when Jesus was teaching in my front room...

Jesus did not have many possessions, probably because of the life he lived. He didn't have a donkey or a camel, so he walked everywhere. When it came time to enter Jerusalem, to celebrate what we later knew was his last Passover on this earth, he had to borrow a colt for His triumphant entry. When he crossed the Sea of Galilee, he borrowed Peter's boat. In fact, he didn't even have a permanent home. When he lived with Mary and Joseph, he lived in Nazareth. Once he started teaching, he didn't have a place to put his pillow. When he stayed in Bethany, he stayed at the home of Martha, Mary, and Lazarus. If he was visiting Peter, he hung his robe there. He was even laid to rest in a borrowed tomb.

One time, when he was in Capernaum for a while, he stayed with me. I was delighted that he wanted to stay with me. When he taught, people came from all over. They flocked to hear him. So many people came to my home that day, it was standing room only. I was so proud that Jesus had come to my house. I was delighted that he had chosen my house to not only stay in, but from which to teach. There, he even taught the teachers of the law!

Then it happened. It started while he was teaching. First, it was just the sounds from the roof. That was bad enough. I didn't want anything to distract people from Jesus' teaching. But there were definitely sounds of scratching from above. Scratching at first, and then clawing. Dust and dirt started to fall on us as we sat and stood inside the room, pressed against the walls. I hoped Jesus would not notice. I would have to check it later. Frankly, I was embarrassed that something was wrong with my roof. I didn't want Jesus to think I had not taken care of everything before he arrived. The sound got louder. Someone was digging through my roof! People were getting distracted from Jesus' teaching and they were getting covered with dirt. I looked apologetically at Jesus, mortified that my home was no longer the perfect setting for his words of wisdom and truth. He kept right on teaching, as if not noticing that the roof was falling in on him. Paralyzed from sheer embarrassment, not knowing quite what to do, I pretended to listen, trying to focus, but every few moments my eyes glanced upward. Every time I looked up dust fell into my eyes. More and more light filtered in as the hole got bigger. Usually I liked to see the way dust danced in beams of light. I did not like it this time. People were starting to cough and choke from the dust. By now, just about everyone was looking up and suddenly four faces appeared, looking down at us, from the edges of the hole. I do not even remember if Jesus had stopped teaching.

The next thing I knew, the room got darker. A disturbance became impossible to ignore when a mat with a man lying on it came through the roof. By this time, all eyes were on the man on the mat. People cleared a space for the mat to rest on the floor. The four men who had lowered him into my house had, by now, come through the door in the traditional manner of entering a house. I am not sure which of us was more befuddled: the man on the mat or myself. He didn't get up. Apparently, he couldn't.

Jesus stopped teaching, and everyone's eyes were on Jesus. That was fortunate. I didn't want them looking at me. Jesus was not looking at me either. That was also good, because I didn't want him to be upset with me that my house was now a full-blown mess, totally unfit for Jesus. Totally unsuitable for a rabbi.

Everyone in the room held their breath. It was only a moment, because Jesus immediately assessed the entire situation: hole in my roof, mess on my floor, paralyzed man and four friends and everyone else staring at him. He said, "Son, your sins are forgiven." I thought Jesus was probably as annoyed with the man on the mat as I was, interrupting Jesus' teaching, let alone destroying my house. Ah, I was so relieved! He wasn't angry with me for my roof falling in. Jesus was dealing with the offense of the five men ruining my roof and interrupting his teaching. So I thought.

The teachers of the law were not happy with what had just happened either. Not the roof mess. They were unhappy with what Jesus said. They weren't saying it out loud. But their annoyance with Jesus was as obvious as my relief that he wasn't mad at me.

Jesus must have known what the teachers of the law were thinking. He asked them "Why are you thinking these things? Which is easier: to say to this paralyzed man, 'Your sins are forgiven,' or to say, 'Get up, take your mat and walk'? But I want you to know that the Son of Man has authority on earth to forgive sins." The next thing I knew, he said to the man on the mat, "I tell you, get up, take your mat and go home." No kidding, the man on the mat got up, took his mat and walked out in front of all of us. He walked out of my house as if it was the most natural thing in the world. Naturally, this amazed everyone and suddenly people praised God, saying, "We have never seen anything like this" (Mark 2:8-12).

Jesus eventually stopped teaching and people went home. Later that day, as Jesus and I cleaned up the mess on my floor, we talked about that hole and the mess in my house. We laughed about it and I had to admit to him that, had he told me about the mess to come when he asked to stay with me, I am not so sure I would have said yes. Sure, I loved having Jesus stay with me in my house. I really loved when he was teaching and people would come and hear him. But that mess!

On that day, he did something more than teach and preach in my house. He stopped the clucking tongues and accusations of the teachers of the law. He healed a man. He answered the prayers of four men whose friend had lived his life on a mat. It required a hole in my roof. It required a temporary mess in my house. That night, as we sat down to eat a simple meal, I thanked Jesus for coming to stay with me and, together, we blessed the mess.

Following at a Distance

LUKE 22:54-62

It is Holy Week. I usually break from reading my *One-Year Bible* at this time and reflect on the passion of Jesus. Every year, it seems, God opens my eyes and heart to something different, something new. It blesses me and delights me when God does that; it is a reminder of how deep, wide, high, long, and broad the richness and beauty of his Word is. So it came as a bit of a surprise to me when the phrase "at a distance" caught my attention the first three days of Holy Week. I just thought it was a little odd. But, it appears twice in the Gospel of Luke, and when God says something twice, I usually listen extra well.

Luke 22:54-62 is the account of Peter who followed "at a distance" as the chief priests, the officers of the temple guard and the elders seized Jesus and led him away to the house of the High Priest. There, as Jesus was interrogated and abused by the Chief Priest, Peter sat by the fire in the courtyard. A servant girl looked at him and said, "This man was with him." Maybe she had seen Peter and Jesus at the market or at the temple when Jesus turned the tables over, or maybe she had seen Peter with Jesus as Jesus rode the colt into Jerusalem. We don't know where or when, but she had seen Peter with Jesus and associated them. *Why,* she may have thought, *wasn't he with Jesus now?*

Shortly thereafter, while Peter was still warming himself at the fire, another person identified Peter as having been with Jesus. Peter answered, "Man, I am not!" And a short time later, someone said, "Certainly this fellow was with him, for he is a Galilean." Peter, according to Matthew 26, answered with oaths and cursing, "I don't know what you are talking about." What follows then is perhaps one of the saddest and most poignant verses in the Bible:

> Just as he was speaking, the rooster crowed. The Lord turned and looked straight at Peter. Then Peter remembered the word the Lord had spoken to him: "Before the rooster crows today, you will disown me three times." And he went outside and wept bitterly. (Luke 22:60-62).

Peter denied him three times. Peter. Peter, the first to confess Jesus as the Christ.

Peter, one of the three disciples taken up to see the Lord Jesus transfigured. Peter, brazen enough to ask to walk on water. Peter, who couldn't decide whether he should let Jesus wash all of him or none of him. Peter, who had been asked to prepare the Passover meal. Peter, who had been asked to come and watch with Jesus in the Garden of Gethsemane. Peter, who boldly drew his sword and cut off Malchus' ear. Peter, who so confidently had declared, "Even if I have to die with you, I will never leave you." Peter, who had seen Jesus raise Lazarus from the dead, seen Jesus heal Jairus' daughter and heal his own mother-in-law. Peter, who had seen him teach the masses, feed the five thousand, and heal blind Bartimaeus. Peter, who had seen miracles, had revelations, and experienced victories with Jesus. But now——now when it counted——Peter followed at a distance.

Why? Why did Peter follow at a distance? It could not have been disinterest; otherwise he would not have followed at all. It was not hatred of Jesus, because remembering Jesus' words and seeing the piercing look of Jesus made Peter weep bitterly. I submit to you that it was fear. Fear made Peter follow at a distance.

Think about it. Things were spinning out of control from the time that Peter lopped off Malchus' ear. It was all so not what Peter wanted or planned. And being out of control usually makes us very, very afraid. Fear caused Peter to follow at a distance.

How often do I do the very same thing? *Yes, Jesus, I can read my Bible, go to my small group, show up at church, but I can't be too close to you right now. It might cost me, it might hurt. Yes, I've seen great things, I've beheld answered prayers. But I just cannot be too close to you. Right now, things are just too painful. Things are too confusing. Things are too difficult. Life is taking too many unexpected turns. Of course I'll follow you, but forgive me if it's at a distance.*

Beloved, this is an odd verse; it isn't exactly a verse most preachers or teachers will "camp on" at Easter. The second time that "at a distance" is used is in Luke 23:47-49:

> The centurion, seeing what had happened, praised God and said, "Surely this was a righteous man." When all the people who had gathered to witness this sight saw what took place, they beat their breasts and went away. But all those who knew him, including the women who had followed him from Galilee, stood at a distance, watching these things.

The centurion saw what happened, had a revelation, and praised God. Even some of the people who had demanded, "Crucify him," saw what happened and beat their breasts. But the women who had walked with him and followed him, stood at a distance and watched. The ones closest to him stood at a distance. Nothing was turning out the way anyone thought it would. Everything was going wrong. And so, maybe it was easier to stand at a distance and watch rather than get too close to Jesus.

Some who may be reading this may see life spinning out of control or feel like everything is going wrong. Nothing is going according to plan. It is easier to stay at a distance. Retreat seems like a safe option, but retreating from Jesus is never a safe option.

Beloved, this is the time to stay close. Draw near, even in the midst of anguish and pain, draw near. It may be Friday, but Sunday is coming.

Right Click: Accept This Invitation

EXODUS 12:41

Just about the time that I learned how to set up calendar invitations on Outlook® and "accept," "decline," or "maybe," my company moved to Google® calendars. It hurts my brain to be reconfigured with advancing technology, but if I want people to consider my schedule and if I want to get on my boss' agenda, I just have to let my brain hurt a little and try to keep up with the ever advancing technology. I also must recognize that if my boss invites me to a meeting, I had better figure out how to accept or decline the invite.

So it is with God's calendar.

"At the end of the 430 years, to the very day, all the LORD's divisions left Egypt" (Exodus 12:41). On that very day, when more than 600,000 people checked their calendars, up popped the reminder window that blared out, "Deliverance from slavery," and in unison they said, "Oh, can't forget that today is the day of God's deliverance from leeks, onions, brick making, pyramid building, beatings, and enslavement. Hello freedom! Goodbye Pharaoh."

To the very day.

What day? Where in the Bible does it say that on this particular day God was going to propel 600,000 plus Israelites out of bondage after 430 years, far from the promised land?

God had promised Abraham and his descendants, "All the land that you see I will give to you and your offspring forever" (Exodus 13:15), meaning Canaan. That implied that any other place they stopped along the way, no matter how long, was not the location of possession. If you have ever bought a house, you know the importance of location, location, and location. The Israelites fled from Canaan to Egypt, lived there, prospered there, fought there. Yet, the promised land was still in their possession. Possession of a place is more than dwelling in a place. Squatters can live someplace, but that place does not belong to the squatter. Someday, God had promised, he would bring the Israelites into the promised land. God said to Abraham, "The whole land of Canaan, where you now reside as a foreigner, I will give as an everlasting possession to you and your descendants after you; and I will be their God" (Genesis 17:8). Likewise, God promised Abraham's grandson Jacob, as he lay on the ground of Canaan, "I will give you and your descendants the land on which you are lying" (Genesis 28:13).

Years later, as Jacob wrestled with the thought of leaving Canaan, longing to be reunited with his son Joseph, but having to go to Egypt, God assured him: "I will go down to Egypt with you, and I will surely bring you back again. And Joseph's own hand will close your eyes" (Genesis 46:4).

From the mouth of Joseph, God again, promised the sons of Jacob, "God will surely come to your aid and take you up out of this land to the land he promised on oath to Abraham, Isaac and Jacob" (Genesis 50:24).

Nowhere in these biblical mile markers did God indicate "and this date will be that very day. You can get it on the calendar." But throughout the lives of Abraham, Isaac, Jacob, Joseph, and then Moses, God made it clear that Canaan—the land where Abraham had been an alien, the land where Jacob had rested his head, the land from which Jacob and seventy members of his family (Genesis 46:26-27) emigrated—was the promised land. In all the time that the Israelites had lived and prospered in Egypt, Egypt never became the promised land. Canaan was. All signs pointed to Canaan. Even in the midst of plenty and in the midst of trial and exile, God's promise stood—someday the promise would become reality.

God also expressed his intention and his will to us in this time. We walk through trial and difficulties. We wander through wildernesses of our own making and God leads us through those wildernesses. Sometimes, we spend years in a place that seems promising, but it turns out not to be the promised land we had hoped for. Yet, God's will prevails. "Many are the plans in a man's heart, but it is the LORD's purpose that prevails" (Proverbs 19:21). This is why Jesus taught his disciples to pray, "Your kingdom come, your will be done on earth as it is in heaven" (Matthew 6:10). God's purpose prevails in his time.

God has a plan and a timetable. And, if we will pay attention, we will see little reminders along the way that that which is foreordained in heaven, that which already is in heaven, will be revealed and accomplished on earth. His will is being worked out as year succeeds year, months follow, until His sovereign, awesome plan is revealed. On that very day. Right click "accept" if you want to be part of that day.

The Herculean Task

EXODUS 16

The dreaded chore chart. And, the worst chore ever for my middle-school aged son, was emptying the dishwasher. One day, I listened to him open and close the dishwasher door several times, slam the plates on the counter, shut cabinet doors just loudly enough so that I knew he was annoyed, and whine about how he did not know where anything went. Pretending to be calm and unaffected, I asked him, "Why do you make this very simple task so hard?" His three-word answer carried more truth and punch than he probably knew: "Because I can." We all get tasks we dislike and sometimes we make them harder, just because we can.

Hercules has the mythological honor of having performed twelve of the most difficult tasks assigned to anyone—kill the Nemean lion, slay the nine-headed hydra, capture and bring back the Erymanthian boar, retrieve the belt of Hippolyta, and several other seemingly impossible tasks—all of which required great courage, skill, strength, cunning, and probably a measure of foolhardiness. He had a strong and compelling reason to pursue and succeed at such tasks: through completing the tasks, he would atone for deeds done while temporarily insane. Surely that was worth facing beasts, dragons, and the elements and risking the rage of the gods of the netherworld.

For the Israelites, there were no twelve tasks. For the Israelites, there was only one task. The task for the Israelites was more difficult, more challenging, and more fraught with danger than anything Hercules faced. Furthermore, unlike Hercules, for whom the place of testing was far from home, for the Israelites, the place of testing and performing the tasks was between their shoulders, in their chest cavity, the heart.

> There the LORD issued a ruling and instruction for them and put them to the test. He said, "If you listen carefully to the LORD your God and do what is right in his eyes, if you pay attention to his commands and keep all his decrees, I will not bring on you any of the diseases I brought on the Egyptians, for I am the LORD, who heals you" (Exodus 15:25-26).

The test is fairly clear: Listen, do what is in right in his eyes, pay attention, and keep his decrees. "Listen" and "pay attention" are pretty much the same thing. "Do what is right in his eyes" and "keep all his decrees" are similar enough to pass as one thing. In short, listen to what God says and do it.

Immediately after the Lord had told them the test, he gave the Israelites Part 1 of the test. The Israelites were enjoying one of their complaining fests; they were remembering with fondness the good ol' days in Egypt when they sat around pots of meat and ate all the food they wanted. (That must have been between the times they were baking bricks and being beaten.)

> Then the LORD said to Moses, "I will rain down bread from heaven for you. The people are to go out each day and gather enough for that day. In this way I will test them and see whether they will follow my

instructions. On the sixth day they are to prepare what they bring in, and that is to be twice as much as they gather on the other days" (Exodus 16:4-5).

And just in case the Israelites did not completely understand, the Lord clarified to Moses, and Moses said to the Israelites:

> "It is the bread the LORD has given you to eat. This is what the LORD has commanded: 'Everyone is to gather as much as they need. Take an omer for each person you have in your tent'" ... Then Moses said to them, "No one is to keep any of it until morning" (Exodus 16:15, 16, 19).

That sounds pretty simple: Gather what you need, no more, no less. That was the instruction. They heard it. The test was to obey, to keep the decree. Simple as it was, some could not pass this test. Some people insisted on gathering extra manna. The next morning the manna they had saved was full of maggots. And if the maggots in the manna wasn't enough, Moses got mad.

A few days later, the Lord promised that before the Sabbath, he would provide enough for the Israelites to gather what they needed per person for two days. He warned that on the Sabbath, they would find neither manna nor quail on the ground. Again, the instruction was clear. But, would the people gather enough for two days or would they go out on the seventh day? Of course some did go out, looking for the manna (Exodus 16:27-29).

So the people rested on the seventh day. Maybe they didn't rest. Maybe they grumbled about the fact that they got up early and there was no manna. Maybe they whined about the fact that Sabbath manna looked and tasted like every day manna. Maybe they murmured about the confusion: do we pick up double today or yesterday? Seventh day from which day? The Lord had spoken. The people had heard, but some simply could not obey and carry out the instructions of the Lord. They made it hard because they could.

The Herculean task for me involves neither boar nor belt nor beast, nor even emptying the dishwasher. My daily task is to simply obey what I hear and not make it harder, just because I can.

Closing the Gap

JOHN 21

There is good news that follows the bad
news of our betrayals, our denials, and our
shame. It is the good news in light of the reality that even as zealous, ardent, and passion-
ate believers, we can, and often do, follow
Jesus at a distance. Then when we are at our
seemingly safe, yet uncomfortable distance,
we feel that piercing gaze. We remember our
bravado, our resolve, and our boldness, and
we weep bitterly.

Who knows where Peter went after
being cowed by a servant girl and adamantly
denying that he had been with Jesus. Maybe
he fled to his boat. In fact, I rather think he

went far from the other disciples. His shame and guilt might have forced him to seek isolation. (Shame and guilt have a way of doing that). If he went to some place where the disciples and he had been with Jesus, perhaps the disciples exchanged how-awful-I-am stories. (Isn't that what we do?) The fact is, when we have disappointed ourselves and our Lord, we want to hide. We get consumed by, "How can he ever forgive me?" So the default thought is, "How can I undo this?"

The beauty of Resurrection Sunday is we can do nothing. But, oh, can God ever do the impossible! Peter's denial and betrayal started with his following at a distance. That denial created a breach, a break, a gap, a chasm in the relationship. Jesus restored it; I call that restoration "closing the gap." It happens in three steps. First, God raised Jesus from the dead. Second, Jesus called for Peter specifically. Third, Jesus had a heart-to-heart conversation with Peter that restored him and renewed him. It really is all about Jesus and, at the same time, it's also all about Peter, because Jesus loves Peter.

No one can describe how God raised Jesus from the dead. No one knows what that looked like. All we know is that afterward, everything was very neat. It's not as if Jesus exploded out of the tomb, although he could have. I don't really picture him as the Incredible Hulk bursting out of his grave clothes and shattering the tomb's opening. God doesn't leave messes. The grave clothes were lying there in the tomb, and the burial cloth that had been around Jesus' head was neatly folded. The stone that had covered the tomb was rolled away.

Somehow between sundown Friday and Sunday morning, Jesus came back to life. That event was critical and crucial to Peter's restoration, yet Peter had nothing to do with it, and no one saw it happen. Peter, like most of us, when he saw the strips of linen, "went away, wondering to himself what had happened" (Luke 24:12).

The second part of the restoration happened when the angel told Jesus' mother Mary, Mary Magdalene, and Salome, "But go, tell his disciples and Peter, 'He is going ahead of you into Galilee'" (Mark 16:7). He could have said, "Go tell those disciples of Jesus..." He could have said, "Tell Peter, who denied me three times, I'm going to really make him pay for that one." He could have said, "Tell anyone who really cares about me and really is serious about following Jesus." But the angel didn't. The angels get their marching orders from God; they say what they're told to say. And this angel was very specific: "Tell the disciples and Peter." That's beautiful. That's merciful. And that's incredible. Jesus wanted Mary to make sure that Peter knew he was alive, just as he had said.

If I want to make sure one of my children in particular gets the message, I single him or her out using their name. It always works. Jesus singled Peter out. Peter was going to get the message: "He has risen! He is going ahead of you into Galilee. There you will see him, just as he told you" (Mark 16:6, 7).

Peter disappears from the narrative for a while. Jesus appears several more times to the disciples, on the road to Emmaus, to all the disciples, and a special appearance for Thomas. Although we have every reason to believe that Peter was present when Jesus appeared to the other disciples, we do not have restoration between Jesus and Peter yet. It takes more than Jesus being raised from the dead, and it takes more than Jesus calling Peter. In fact, it is a week, another appearance, and a special conversation before restoration occurs.

It happened on the beach and is recorded in John 21. It's really quite amazing because Peter knows Jesus is alive, risen from the dead, just as he said. But he clearly has no idea what he is supposed to do with that piece of remarkable information. So, being Peter, he declares, "I'm going out to fish." I sort of imagine Peter thinking to himself, I may not know what to do with Jesus, but I do know how to fish! Of course, he catches nothing. Jesus, standing on the shore watching all this unfold, suggests a better fishing hole, and John recognizes Jesus immediately. Peter jumps into the water (no walking on water for him this time) and wades to Jesus. "They knew it was the Lord" (John 21:12). And here Jesus initiates the most critical conversation Peter would ever have: "Simon, son of John, do you love me more than these?" (John 21:15). The question probably took Peter's breath away because it might have reminded him of his fervent declaration, "Even if all fall away on account of you, I never will.

Even if I have to die with you, I will never disown you" (Matthew 26:33, 35). In Jesus' three questions, Peter knew Jesus was recounting the three denials.

This was not a case of Jesus rubbing salt in Peter's wounds; it was Jesus dealing with Peter's guilt and shame and taking it away, every painful and bitter piece of it. That is how the gap has to be closed; that is how we are restored: by letting Jesus initiate, letting him lay before us our guilt and shame, and allowing him to take it away.

There was nothing Peter could do to close the gap. Nothing in his human, fleshly arsenal would ever make up for following at a distance and for denying and betraying Jesus three times. It takes a God who raises Jesus from the dead. It takes a God who calls us by name and says, "I want you to know I'm alive and I did just what I said I would do." It takes a God who sits on the shore with us and commissions us to love and feed his lambs.

On Good Friday I discovered that like the disciples, I follow at a distance because it is simply too painful to stay close to Jesus; I get afraid. I have more in common with my friend Peter than I like to admit. However, Saturday morning I let him take away my guilt and my shame and Jesus and I had a little heart-to-heart. You see, he still closes the gap for each one of us. Whether it is Peter or you or me, we all at times follow at a distance. And God through Jesus, in his grace and mercy, comes in gentle power, calls us by name, and restores us. He calls us to come close and have a little breakfast fish and tête-à-tête.

Everyday is Resurrection Day for Christians. Hallelujah, he is risen indeed!

Don't Leave Me Alone

DEUTERONOMY 31:8

Marcia and I first went to Europe together when I was a freshman in college and she was a junior. We went during January term and hit several countries—Holland to visit relatives, Germany to visit our sister, Belgium to visit mutual friends, and Spain to visit a friend of Marcia's. True story: The last thing our father said to us in his thick Dutch accent before we boarded the plane was a cautionary, "Don't go to Madrid. It is very unstable." What did it matter that he was in international banking and had traveled the world? What did it matter if he had more traveling experience in his back pocket than we did in our suitcases and knapsacks put together? We were young. Translate: invincible (or stupid). So we, of course, traveled through Madrid on our way to the northern coast of Spain. Wouldn't you know as we sipped our cold drinks in a Spanish café in Madrid waiting for the through train, armed soldiers appeared at every street corner. Yes, he was right. A coup was happening right before our eyes. But I digress.

So, having had such a great time, we went to Europe again after I finished graduate school. We traveled well together. She was always fun, yet cautious. I was fun, and reckless. And because we were both Christians, we prayed a lot together. We prayed a lot when those armed soldiers showed up outside the café. Another time, we were in Paris riding the metro to the train station during rush hour. We got separated. This was in the days before cell phones. We had no sou or centimes and could not speak French. I was the one on the train clinging to the pole as the doors closed between us. I don't know about Marcia, but I was praying my guts out. Somehow, I knew enough to get off at the next train station, I spied her as her train rolled in and got on the train. We laughed the rest of the way to our destination.

Many years later, I went to Europe for work. Although, dear, sweet Marcia, had been diagnosed with the illness that cannot be named, I decided I would take her with me. We would have fun. We would laugh and pray a lot. My husband, Phil, and two sons also went, but I really wanted Marcia with me. I wanted to visit elderly relatives one more time and see some of the sights we saw when we were young and fun. I spoke with her, as I tried to every other day, even for only ten minutes, lest there be the day when I can no longer do so. I said excitedly, "Marsh, we got the tickets. We are all set for our trip." Her response was a little flat as I enthused about Belgium and Holland, maybe Paris.

"Marsh, are you excited?"

"Yes, I am. But I am a little nervous."

And then, because one of my desires in life now is to protect her and take care of her, as she always tried to do for me when we were both fun but I was reckless and she was cautious, I slowed down. "Well, what are you nervous about, and let's see how we can take care of that."

"Well, you know I get nervous when I go anywhere different."

"Yes, I know, but you have been to all these places before. And we are going to see people you know and who love you and you love them." Silence from Marcia.

"I know. But I get nervous. Just don't leave me alone."

"Marsh, I am not going to leave you alone at all. Phil is going, too, and he or I will always be with you. I am not going to leave you."

"Okay then. Then I will be excited and not nervous."

At that moment, a lightness and tangible relief moved into her voice and demeanor. I could feel it even through the phone. I remembered another time when I was traveling alone to Thailand sometime between the trip to Europe with Marcia and the upcoming trip. We were sitting in her living room; I was probably holding her baby, Nicholas, and she asked me if I was scared.

"No, a little nervous though."

"What are you nervous about?"

"What am I not nervous about?" I laughed, because I was still fun but a little less reckless. "I am nervous about being alone and nervous about doing dumb things." I had a great idea: "Hey, do you want to go with?"

"Well, no, I don't think Nicholas would like that much. But I will be praying for you every day. And the Lord says he will never leave you or forsake you. So you won't be alone. And, maybe you don't need to be nervous."

As always, she was right.

And for Marcia, this is a different journey altogether. Not the journey to Europe, the other one. And we are both nervous, as are all of us who love dear, sweet Marcia. But I remember what Marcia told me when I was headed to Thailand: the Lord says he will never leave or forsake you. We won't be alone and maybe, just maybe, neither of us needs to be nervous. And Marcia and I would still be fun, both cautious and both praying.

Our Small Part

EXODUS 35-36

I went to one of my husband's work events yesterday. They were expecting to feed 400 people. That is a lot of food for typically ravenous students celebrating one of their favorite national holidays. The staff had been planning this event for about five months. A lot of detailing, planning, asking for donations of food, gifts, prizes and recruiting of willing servers and volunteers happened in between the day the date of the event was determined and the actual event. It is one of the four or five signature events for the organization and many students leave the event feeling very loved and the volunteers leave the event tired but thrilled to have been able to be part of the outreach.

Building the sanctuary was one of God's signature events in his history with Israel. It starts out months before the event actually happens. In chapters 24 through 32 of Exodus, God and Moses have a forty-day retreat on Mount Sinai. There, on the mountain, the Lord gave Moses not only the Ten Commandments but a blueprint, a design, for the sanctuary that the people of Israel were supposed to build (Exodus 24:8-9). The Lord gave to Moses, in great detail, the plans for the place of worship, its construction, and all of its furnishings. Nothing was missing. And when they had completed the sanctuary, God would dwell among the Israelites (Exodus 25:8).

But how would such a task be accomplished? The design and blueprints specified hides of sea cows, gold, bronze, acacia wood, oil of pressed olives, and blue, purple and scarlet yarn. The list goes on and on. And not in small quantities! The sanctuary was not to be a scale model; the sanctuary was to be approximately 100 x 50 cubits (150 x 75 feet). Constructing it would be no small feat. How was God going to provide the resources and supplies and the labor and craftsmen to do it?

Ironically, part of the resources came from the people of Egypt themselves, since God had instructed Moses to tell the people of Israel to ask the Egyptians for gifts and promised he would go before the Israelites and predispose the Egyptians, who hated the Israelites, to give generously. And it was so.

The Israelites plundered the Egyptians.

Great start! But what about the construction?

> "So Bezalel, Oholiab and every skilled
> person to whom the LORD has given
> skill and ability to know how to carry out
> all the work of constructing the sanctuary
> are to do the work just as the LORD has
> commanded." Then Moses summoned
> Bezalel and Oholiab and every skilled
> person to whom the LORD had given
> ability and who was willing to come and
> do the work (Exodus 36:1-2).

This is a wonderful picture of how God calls his people to provide the resources of skill, ability, and knowledge for his biggest projects and plans.

The only thing left for the people of Israel to provide was willingness.

The word "willing" is used no less than six times in chapters 35 and 36 of Exodus.

Exodus 35:5 describes a people who heard the summons of Moses: "From what you have, take an offering for the Lord. Everyone who is willing is to bring to the Lord an offering..." From that point on, in Exodus 35:21-29, we see a great parade of Israelites coming to participate with willing hearts: everyone, men and women, those who had linen, yarn, acacia wood, onyx stones.

This kind of outpouring of willingness in God's people is moved by the Spirit of God. It is as though people were climbing over each other to give, to participate in what God was doing among his people. God provided the resources. God provided the skill and the ability. His people brought the willingness.

Last night, as I weaved my way through

the line to fill my plate with all the donated yummy food, I thanked the volunteer server and asked if he had eaten yet. He hadn't, but he flashed me a huge smile, touched his heart and said "My heart is full. I am just happy to be here."

God provides the plans and the designs. Moved by his Holy Spirit, we, his people, bring the willingness to participate in his signature events. We touch our hearts and say, "My heart is full. I am just happy to be here."

The End of the Beginning

ECCLESIASTES 7:8

I love to read. Sometimes I have to read all the way to the end of the story to figure out the beginning. Sometimes I understand the beginning, but it isn't until I get to the end that I comprehend the significance of the beginning. Then, I get to the end of the story, experience the "aha" moment, and realize, "Wow, I never could have seen this coming from that inauspicious beginning." Likewise, I don't think I could have foreseen this essay serving as the end of the beginning.

Once upon a time I was in the fourth grade.

Mrs. Drachman had been renamed Mrs. Dracula by those of us in her fourth grade at the Mary Lyon School in Boston. Of course, we were brave enough to call her that only on the playground; we were so clever! Mrs. Dracula probably had a little bit of the terrifying in her from a fourth grader's perspective. However, in hindsight, she did get some things right.

One day, she gave us a typical elementary school assignment, meant to challenge our growing minds to think beyond the spatial bounds of the playground and the time bounds of recess. The assignment was to write an essay about what we wanted to be when we grew up. Although I remember nothing about the why or the wherefore, I remember distinctly articulating for the first time in my ten years of life that I wanted to be an author. I finished the essay in a timely fashion and let my parents read it. Their reaction, perhaps birthed out of their immigrant intense desire for financial security or perhaps born out of their desire that their children have letters after their names, was "You will never make a living that way. Choose something else."

Like any good ten-year old, I heard their words and sensed the gross error of my thinking and the stupidity of choosing a career that would most certainly never yield "a living." I could feel the gravitas of their stern words. I could feel it, but I could not understand why making a living was so important, how it was supposed to happen, and why on earth it should matter to me. Nonetheless, the message was clear: my choice was a mistake. Being an author would never gain my parents' approval. I was defeated before my first rejection letter.

My career choice got shoved underground, and I never spoke of it again to my parents. I silently found pleasure playing with words, wrote smarmy poetry that mercifully has not been kept, faithfully kept a journal most of my adult life, and loved articulating ideas with words that made other people light up with understanding. However, that ten-year-old's conviction that words matter and ideas are important, was true. Words are important, not only to myself as self-expression, but as expression to others. Words are part of my life, to the expression of God in me, to me and through me.

That evening, when my parents disapproved my desire to write, it was too late to obey their command to pick something else and write about it. I reluctantly turned the essay in, certain that I would fail the assignment. After all, Mrs. Dracula was an adult. She, too, would see the obvious stupidity of my choice. I lived in terror: my house was not one into which I could bring an assignment with a low grade.

Mrs. Dracula returned my paper with only one comment accompanying the A−: "Nicely written. You are on your way."

Now, 45 years later, I wish I could say two things to Mrs. Drachman:

I am very sorry I called you Mrs. Dracula. I am finally on my way.

Acknowledgments

"I can no other answer make but thanks,
and thanks; and ever thanks"
Twelfth Night, Act III, Scene 3
William Shakespeare

I had the good fortune to not experience any contractions until the night I actually went into labor. This was good and bad. The good part was that I lived a blissful and ignorant nine months. The bad part was that I didn't think it would be as painful to birth a child as everyone kept telling me about their experiences in the labor and delivery room. When those contractions finally did come, I was a little ... um, hysterical. Fortunately, my very calm husband drove me. The receptionist got me a wheelchair. When I said, "I'm done, it's time for me to go home," the nurse firmly held me down and said "Mrs. Foell, we need you to be present for us to have this baby." About forty-five minutes after getting wheeled into the labor and delivery room, our first child crowned and presented herself to her audience. Tada!

Writing and publishing a book is very much like pregnancy. I can now say I have done both, so I speak from experience. It takes more than one person to birth a book. Therefore, although I never thanked the attendant who sped me into labor and delivery or the nurse for her calm and logical response that helped me birth a child, I need to thank some people for helping me birth a book.

Thank you, Karen Oliver and Rebecca Faith, who edited the manuscript patiently, encouraging me every step of the way.

Thank you, Terri Fox, who regularly met with me and gently pushed me, quietly asking, "How is your book coming?" Terri read through individual essays as well as the entire manuscript with the skillful eyes and tender heart of a friend and writer. I owe you a breakfast.

Thank you, Chris and Judy Schenk, who have coached my husband and me through some difficult transitions. It was only natural to call on them to help me birth this book. The transition from writing to actually publishing can be overwhelming, and Chris and Judy firmly told me to stay present in the midst of the transition.

Thank you, Firepond Press, for being willing to take a chance on me and publish the book.

Thank you, Phil, my dear husband, and who really is the love of my life, who made room in the midst of our very busy and full lives and encouraged me to find space and time to fulfill my desire and calling to write.

Thank you, Deborah, our oldest child, who sat down and wrote a biography for me when I was stuck at "I was born in a small apartment in Amsterdam."

Thank you, Sam, our older son (by six minutes), who took up photography in the nick of time and agreed to take my picture, if I gave him the photo credit.

Thank you to my other two wonderful children, Anna and Paul, and my extended family, who have, intentionally or unintentionally, invited me into their lives. In, and

through, our precious relationships and experiences, I have learned that everyday Truth
matters.

FIREPOND

PRESS

Made in the USA
Coppell, TX
07 August 2021

60108109R10144